WHO DELIBERATES?

Bruce —
An effort at
story telling Ben

AMERICAN POLITICS AND POLITICAL ECONOMY
A SERIES EDITED BY BENJAMIN I. PAGE

BENJAMIN I. PAGE

Who Deliberates?

Mass Media in Modern Democracy

THE UNIVERSITY OF CHICAGO PRESS

Chicago & London

BENJAMIN I. PAGE is the Gordon Scott Fulcher Professor of Decision Making in the Department of Political Science at Northwestern University. Of his six previous books, two have been published by the University of Chicago Press—*Choices and Echoes in Presidential Elections* (1978) and *The Rational Public* (1992).

The University of Chicago Press, 60637
The University of Chicago Press, Ltd., London
© 1996 by The University of Chicago
All rights reserved. Published 1996
Printed in the United States of America
05 04 03 02 01 00 99 98 97 96   1 2 3 4 5

ISBN (cloth): 0-226-64472-3
ISBN (paper): 0-226-64473-1

Library of Congress Cataloging-in-Publication Data

Page, Benjamin I.
    Who deliberates? : mass media in modern democracy / Benjamin
I. Page.
        p.   cm. — (American politics and political economy)
    Includes bibliographical references (p.   ) and index.
    Contents: Public deliberation and democracy — The New York times
goes to war with Iraq — Assigning blame for the Los Angeles riots –
Zoe Baird, nannies, and talk radio — Conclusion : successes and
failures of mediated deliberation.
    1. Mass media—Political aspects—United States.   2. Communication
in politics—United States.   3. Mass media—Objectivity.
    4. Democracy.   5. United States—Politics and government—1993–
I. Title.   II. Series
P95.82.U6P34   1996
302.23'0973—dc20   95-26652
                                                                        CIP

Preface

In *The Rational Public* (1992), Robert Shapiro and I argued that Americans' collective policy preferences are generally stable, coherent, and sensible, and that public deliberation often works well to enlighten public opinion. At the same time, however, we maintained that the public can sometimes be fooled, deceived, or manipulated by what is printed and broadcast in the mass media. This book explores more fully just how deliberation works through the media. In particular, it investigates under what circumstances the public is enlightened, and when it is fooled, by media-transmitted discussion of political issues. It asks under what conditions modern, mediated public deliberation works well or works badly for democracy.

The book is intended for several audiences. For general readers and students it is written as simply and clearly as I could manage, and I hope that the case studies (presented mainly in narrative, storytelling form) will prove entertaining as well as informative. Political scientists, political sociologists, and others interested in democratic theory and political communication constitute another prime audience. Professional journalists and specialists in media studies will find some familiar and well-established ideas here, given concrete (and, I hope, striking) illustration, and given new meaning by their placement in the context of democratic theory. Specialists will also find some new ideas and new evidence about such matters as how political discourse travels quickly through and across a variety of different media; what roles in deliberation are played by editorials, op-ed columns, and letters to the editor; how editorial and news materials are sometimes connected; and how certain newspapers sometimes become influential political actors, not just passively reporting what others say but acting on their own to shape political debate.

Technical issues and discussions of the scholarly literature are largely relegated to endnotes, which—for the sake of those who hate to flip back and forth—are designed to be readable as a block after each chapter. Scholars and media professionals are urged to read these endnotes; they clarify definitions and methods, elaborate upon theoretical debates, and help indicate what is novel or controversial here. Other readers may wish to skip the notes altogether or just consult them on a few points of particular interest.

The book proceeds as follows. The first chapter outlines some theoretical considerations concerning deliberation and democracy and raises questions to be addressed. Then chapters 2 through 4 discuss three specific cases—the "War," "Riots," and "Nannies" cases—that illuminate these matters. Finally, chapter 5 uses the cases and some additional material to pull together concluding ideas about mediated deliberation and democracy.

This book was researched and written entirely at Northwestern University. Northwestern's excellent research environment, including the library and computer resources drawn upon here, and its outstanding faculty members in Communication Studies, Political Science, and other departments, were extremely helpful. Readers will have to judge the results for themselves, but any virtues of the book owe a great deal to the intellectual environment in which it was produced.

I am grateful to many colleagues at Northwestern and elsewhere who generously took the time to comment on one or more chapters, in one or another version. They include, by chapter and roughly in chronological order: (on chap. 2) Christopher Jencks, Jane Mansbridge, Fay Cook, Tim Fedderson, James Schwoch, William Dorman, Sara Monoson, Noam Chomsky, Anthony Lewis, Andrew Rojecki, Eric Alterman, Daniel Chomsky, Scott Althaus, and Matthew Holden; (on chap. 3) Bob Entman, Susan Herbst, David Protess, Jenny Mansbridge, Daniel Chomsky, Jim Schwoch, Tom Ferguson, Bob Shapiro, Lance Bennett, Erik Devereux, Scott Althouse, Todd Schaefer, Dean Burnham, Sara Monoson, Tom Goodnight, and David Zarefsky; (on chap. 4), Susan Herbst, Daniel Chomsky, Tom Ferguson, Scott Althaus,

David Protess, Hope Ehrman, Sara Monoson, Barbara Sinclair, Arthur Stinchcombe, Lawrence Lichty, Patti Conley, Dennis Chong, and participants in the American Politics Workshop at Northwestern.

I am particularly indebted to Philip Powlick, who first suggested juxtaposing these three cases for a Walker Lecture at DePauw University; and to Bruce Stinebrickner, Keith Nightenhelser, Robert Calvert, and other faculty members and students at DePauw, who, in the course of a remarkably intense day of discussions, helped me see more clearly a number of connections among the public, the mass media, and democracy.

Special thanks to Jason Tannenbaum, who coauthored (and, indeed, conceived and carried out most of the research for) chapter 4; to Jenny Mansbridge and Sara Monoson, who offered many suggestions on democratic theory and deliberation; to Bob Entman and Susan Herbst, who tutored me extensively in communication theory but should not be blamed for the remaining inadequacies of their pupil; to James Crawford, for his expertise in methods of inquiry; and to John Tryneski, for his outstanding editorial work on this and other projects.

As always, I am very grateful to my family, especially Mary, my sharpest but also most supportive critic, and Eleanor, a source, at age twelve, of insights into *Time* magazine, the *Wall Street Journal*, and the mysteries of the information superhighway.

Benjamin I. Page

ONE

Public Deliberation
and Democracy

Public deliberation is essential to democracy, in order to ensure that the public's policy preferences—upon which democratic decisions are based—are informed, enlightened, and authentic.[1] In modern societies, however, public deliberation is (and probably must be) largely *mediated*, with professional communicators rather than ordinary citizens talking to each other and to the public through mass media of communications.

The mediated nature of deliberation raises some potentially troubling questions. Do professional communicators effectively act for, or represent, the public as a whole? What happens if they are seriously unrepresentative in their beliefs, preferences, or values? What if professional communicators purvey misleading information or fail to communicate ideas and information the public needs? Will citizens be deceived? Can the public be misled into supporting policies inconsistent with objective realities or with citizens' basic values and interests?[2]

WHY DELIBERATION IS ESSENTIAL

One of the core ideas of democracy is that governments ought to do what their citizens want them to do. Or, to put it another way, governments ought to pay attention to public opinion, ought to respond to the policy preferences of the people. I am a strong believer in democracy.[3] In *The Rational Public*, Robert Shapiro and I argued that—despite the fears of some of the Founding Fathers like Alexander Hamilton, and contrary to warnings from pundits and scholars like Walter Lippmann—Americans' collective policy preferences are actually well worth paying attention to. Public opinion is generally coherent and consistent. It flows from Americans' basic values, and it is mostly sensible—sometimes more sensible than the views of those who set themselves up as leaders or experts. Public opinion is usually stable, as well, except that it reacts in reasonable ways to world events and to new information that is presented to it.[4]

But there's the rub. Even if the public is capable of a high level of rationality and good sense, public opinion is bound to depend, in good part, upon the political information and ideas that are conveyed to it. If that information is sufficiently full, accurate, and well interpreted, then citizens can decide what policies they want in an informed way, consistent with their basic values and interests. Then it makes sense to insist that government act accordingly. Democracy can work well. But if the information provided to the public is inaccurate, incomplete, misleading, or full of outright lies, then perhaps even a rational public can be fooled. People might be misled into favoring policies that harm themselves and their neighbors, or policies that violate their deepest values. In that event, democracy would not work at all well: government would either have to respond to the public's inauthentic preferences and do harm, or ignore them and violate popular sovereignty.

Democratic theorists have stressed the importance of providing the public with good information and high-quality political *deliberation* (that is, reasoning and discussion about the merits of public policy).[5] Since policymaking is complicated and full of uncertainties, an individual citizen's personal experience and reflection, alone, can get her or him only so far. Sound political judgment requires exchanging knowledge and ideas with others. John Dewey wrote persuasively of the need for a system of "effective and organized inquiry," and for communication by which knowledge is "published, shared, socially accessible," so that it becomes a "common possession" of the members of the public. Only then will an "organized, articulate Public" come into being. Only then can democracy come into its own.[6]

THE FACE-TO-FACE IDEAL

What sort of deliberation does the public need in a democracy? Many exemplars of deliberation, and many of the ideals and normative standards that we associate with it, are based on situations involving face-to-face talk among small numbers of people.

The Assemblies of ancient Athens, for example, where all citizens had equal rights to attend and to speak, and where norms encouraged "frank speaking" and serious listening, involved at most a few thousand individuals.[7] Eighteenth-century salons and coffee houses, which helped inspire Habermas's concepts of the "public sphere" and the "ideal speech situation," involving open and unconstrained public argument and reasoning among equal citizens, were even smaller.[8] Also small are New England town meetings and contemporary clubs and groups, which rely heavily upon feelings of community, friendship, and intimacy when they discuss the issues, then decide by consensus or majority rule.[9]

Similarly, many theories of deliberation have dealt with legislative bodies, where small numbers of legislators, in committees or floor debate, can talk face-to-face, draw upon one another's expertise, and reason about the merits of alternative public policies.[10]

Even some contemporary accounts of "deliberative public opinion" assume that citizens, in order to form well-reasoned opinions, need to meet and discuss the issues in specially assembled small groups.[11] Indeed, some theorists believe that effective deliberation can occur *only* within small, face-to-face groups of people.[12]

THE REALITY: DIVISION OF LABOR

But we know that it is impossible to carry on thorough, face-to-face deliberation among the whole collectivity of millions of citizens who make up the public in a large, complex, modern society like the United States.

The problem is not so much the geographical size of the country or the widespread dispersion of its population, which (in the days of slow transportation and sluggish communication) used to make it hard for citizens to get together. Now everything is faster and closer. It would be possible, at least in principle, for every citizen to sit in front of a two-way video system and make contact with every other citizen at once, in a virtual assembly hall.

The really serious problem—probably an insuperable problem—is the large number of citizens who would have to interact with each other. Even if we were, as AT&T puts it, "all connected," we could not all converse together simultaneously. Modern technology can enable millions of people to listen to a single speaker, all at the same time, but the limits of human attention mean that only one speaker at a time can be listened to by everyone else. If each citizen got equal time to speak to the whole public, she or he would have a very small share of time or a very long wait before it came. If, for example, a nation of 250 million citizens devoted twenty-four hours to fully equal collective discussion of some political issue, each citizen would get less than .0004—less than four ten-thousandths—of one second to talk. If each citizen insisted, instead, upon a rather modest two minutes of speaking time, the discussion would take five hundred million minutes: that is, 347,222 days, or 950 years. Extreme boredom and impatience would result. Little productive work would get done; soon (barring a fully robotic world) the economy would collapse and the deliberators would run out of food to eat.[13]

In order to avoid such absurdities, only a limited number of people can actually speak to the whole public. We must either decentralize deliberation drastically (that is, carry it out in many separate small groups of citizens), or we must accept a division of labor: that is, delegate the jobs of studying policy and addressing the public to a small set of representatives or surrogate deliberators, perhaps to professional policy experts and communicators. In practice, we both decentralize and delegate deliberation.

A second major problem is the great extent and complexity of political problems in modern societies. The broad role of the modern state and the extreme complexity of today's political problems mean that political deliberation must cover a wide variety of matters, each taking a great deal of time and energy. Twenty-four hours of talk is not enough to work out the intricate provisions of an international trade agreement, or to estimate the macroeconomic effects of raising interest rates, or to assess the workings of a proposed welfare reform. When political problems are many and complex, it would take too much time for each citizen to become knowledgeable about the details of all of them. It is necessary for people to specialize, to become experts on particular issues: perhaps for some of them to become paid experts, whose regular jobs involve studying the ins and outs of public policy.

These two features of modern societies, taken together—the large numbers of citizens and the many complex political problems—almost certainly necessitate a *division of labor* in political expertise, policymaking, and communication. This is why we have professional policy experts, at universities, research organizations, and elsewhere, who deliberate about policy in a multitude of small groups of their own. It is also why we have professional politicians and why we have a representative, rather than direct, democracy. The idea is that legislators and other public officials specialize in policymaking and learn a lot about it; they are chosen and held accountable by the citizens they represent.[14]

But the same need for division of labor also applies to political communication. A vigorous democracy cannot settle for a passive citizenry that merely chooses leaders and then forgets entirely about politics. Such a citizenry would not know what it wanted its public officials to do or what they were actually doing. An ignorant public would have no way to hold its officials to account. There would be a very attenuated sort of democracy, if any sort at all. In order that the public as a whole can actively control what its government does, the public, collectively, must be well informed. Some kind of effective *public* deliberation is required that involves the citizenry as a whole.

This suggests the need for *professional communicators,* who not only help policy experts communicate with each other, but also assemble, explain, debate, and disseminate the best available information and ideas about public policy, in ways that are accessible to large audiences of ordinary citizens. That is what Dewey had in mind with his "published, shared, socially accessible" knowledge, and his "subtle, delicate, vivid and responsive art of communication."[15]

In modern societies, of course, public deliberation is in fact highly mediated in just this way.[16] We have mass media of communications, based on print and electronic technologies and on large-scale commercial organization, that enable communicators to reach enormous audiences through mass-circulation newspapers and magazines, radio, and especially television.

Most citizens get most of their political information through such media, supplemented and amplified to varying degrees by personal experience and by conversations with friends, neighbors, and coworkers. Because airtime and print space are extremely expensive, and because citizens want only the most concise and vivid messages, most of those who speak in or through the media are professional communicators, highly skilled at producing political discourse and paid to do so. These professional communicators include reporters, writers, commentators, and television pundits, as well as public officials and selected experts from academia or think tanks.[17]

But professional communicators are not generally elected by the citizenry. Most media are organized as private, profit-seeking businesses.[18] Many professional communicators are employees of those businesses, who may be hired for reasons other than purely to please or inform the average citizen. It seems possible that journalists, experts, media owners and managers, and other professional communicators (even public officials) could have values and interests at odds with those of the general public. This raises a crucial question: *how well do professional communicators represent and serve the public?* Do they convey information and ideas the public needs for developing informed policy preferences? Or do they, to a significant extent, mislead citizens and distort public opinion?

CRITICISMS AND DEFENSES OF THE MEDIA

Some students of the mass media have argued that the media—especially television—fail to serve the public well because they do not provide enough political information. They devote far more time and space to entertainment than to political matters, and political news is usually superficial and incomplete. It tends to ignore historical and factual background and to be fragmented, overly dramatic, and overly personalized.[19]

But defenders of the media answer that, while some or all of this may be true, it doesn't really matter. Of course most people most of the time want entertainment, not politics. But plenty of information is available on CNN or PBS or C-Span or in specialized publications when people want it. Alternatively, citizens can get political information indirectly, by listening to opinion leaders they trust who read elite newspapers like the *New York Times*, the *Wall Street Journal*, or the *Washington Post*, or who keep up with journals of opinion like the *National Review* or the *Nation*. In other words, if extensive political information is available somewhere in the system, not everyone has to pay attention to it all the time; a lot of information, and reasonable conclusions from it, will trickle out through opinion leaders and cue givers to ordinary citizens,[20] who can deliberate about it in their own small, face-to-face groups of family, friends, and co-workers.[21]

I find this answer largely convincing. I believe it is one of the reasons there can be a rational public, with collective policy preferences that respond well to events and new information, even though most individuals do not have a lot of detailed political knowledge. People can and do follow well-informed opinion leaders whom they trust, who encapsulate the fruits of scholarship and expertise; they can and do draw upon their own experience and common sense; and they test their judgments against those of friends and neighbors. Thus the public as a whole can generally form policy preferences that reflect the best available information.[22]

For this reason, I believe we should judge the role of the mass media in a somewhat different way than some scholars do. We should not study only what does or does not appear about politics in just one type of medium, like television news; as far as possible, we should look at what *all* the media have to say, including elite newspapers and journals of opinion, as well as more popular communications channels. We need to pay attention to the totality of political information that is made available, because much of it may make its way, directly or indirectly, to the public.

What about the criticism that the media are much too negative about public officials and political candidates: that they irresponsibly spread gossip and falsehoods, and that scandal has been institutionalized by the practices of "feeding frenzies" and "junk-yard-dog journalism"?[23] Such practices must be taken seriously; they can be unfair to the reputations of public servants, disruptive of elections, and corrosive of citizens' general trust in government. Again, however, they do not necessarily undermine the quality of deliberation about particular public policies, especially if (as I suspect) citizens are usually able—eventually— to sort out titillating speculation from serious evidence of wrongdoing.

Perhaps more disturbing are charges that the media are ideologically biased: that reporters and journalists tend to be liberal—in particular, hostile to the military and to nuclear energy, friendly to environmentalism and to civil rights and liberties;[24] or that the media tend to print and air predominantly conservative views, especially supporting business against labor, and opposing economic regulation, social-welfare policies, and leftist dissent;[25] or that the media are heavily nationalistic, propagating the government line on issues of foreign policy.[26] Although such charges are controversial (ideological bias is notoriously difficult to define or measure),[27] one might expect that, if the media regularly favored values and opinions that were markedly unrepresentative of average citizens' views, the public might be led astray from its genuine interests and values.

Defenders of the media, however, and classical advocates of free speech like John Stuart Mill and Oliver Wendell Holmes, would answer that even ideological bias in the media may not badly distort public deliberation. The crucial factors, according to classical liberals, are *competition* and *diversity*. Let opposing views contend vigorously in the marketplace of ideas; the true will defeat the false. So long as there exist some competing elites who share the values of various groups of citizens, the citizens can rely on cues from those they trust and form sensible judgments, even if the contents of the media are somewhat unbalanced and unrepresentative.[28]

This argument has a great deal of merit. Ordinary people are surprisingly skillful at spotting the truth and rejecting nonsense. The average citizen has a good chance of arriving at sound opinions, so long as good information is available somewhere, and so long as there is vigorous competition among different ideas and interpretations, even if the media are full of bias or contaminated by untruths. Given a few helpful voices, the public as a whole has sometimes formed sensible collective policy preferences even in the face of propaganda campaigns or media-propagated falsehoods.[29]

Still, we should not be beguiled by the economic metaphor of a marketplace of ideas into assuming that the media automatically provide citizens with exactly the ideas and information they need, just as supermarkets are supposed to provide the groceries that consumers want. For one thing, even in markets that work perfectly, producers respond to those who have dollars to spend ("effective demand"), not to equally weighted citizens. The production of political information is therefore likely to tilt toward those (e.g., high-income citizens and large corporations) who can most easily pay for it. This tendency is probably exacerbated by the fact that markets for information generally do not work perfectly, because information is a *public good*. It is very hard selectively to exclude people from getting information, and therefore hard to make people pay for it—especially information that would help large, dispersed groups of citizens. Thus there is little money to be made by producing such information, and it is probably underproduced relative to the political knowledge and/or propaganda bought by businesses and other concentrated interests.

While these likely antidemocratic biases in the information system may be quite important, direct evidence about them is hard to come by, and what we will be able to say about them is limited. Of more immediate relevance to the concerns of this book are two other ways in which the market in political information can fail and competition and diversity of ideas can collapse: through monopoly government control of information (especially foreign-policy information), and through duopoly control by the two major political parties, which may sometimes agree with each other and respond to financial investors rather than to ordinary citizens.[30]

For example, public deliberation may be harmed because the media rely heavily upon *official sources* for news stories and perhaps for commentary as well.[31] It is perfectly reasonable for the media to pay attention to public officials. But if official sources dominate or overwhelm other voices in political deliberation, if an official point of view is conveyed but other important views are excluded, citizens may be misled. This seems especially likely to happen in foreign affairs, where government officials sometimes have a high degree of control over relevant information—even monopoly control—and may be tempted to suppress or distort what they know. Such suppression or distortion has occurred in some important cases, including the Tonkin

Gulf incident at the beginning of the Vietnam War, the imaginary "window of vulnerability" to Soviet missiles in the 1970s and early 1980s, and various other international crises and covert operations, as well as certain domestic matters like nuclear-energy policy.[32]

Similarly, a two-party political system contributes to the illusion that there are two and only two sides to every issue, and tends to stifle dissent. Furthermore, not even two sides may actually be presented. Competition for electoral victory tends to drive the two parties to take stands that are rather similar to each other. To the extent that both parties appeal to the median (average) voter, this can facilitate a democratic electoral outcome: the winner will stand for popular policies.[33] At the same time, however, this competitive pressure tends to reduce the diversity of political ideas and information available to the public. Worse yet, in some cases both parties may take similar stands that respond to campaign contributors rather than to ordinary voters, leaving large groups of citizens with no helpful political voice at all to listen to.[34] Then both the Republicans and the Democrats may fail to communicate important information that the public needs. This may have happened, for example, in the savings-and-loan debacle of the 1980s, and in the crusades for deficit cutting and international free trade in the early 1990s.

An additional problem (perhaps related to the high-income information biases discussed above) is that, in certain respects, nearly all communications professionals—even elected public officials—may be unrepresentative of American citizens as a whole and may not share ordinary citizens' values. For example, the most prominent journalists, television commentators, and public officials tend to have much higher incomes than the average American and to live in very different circumstances. On certain class-related issues, it seems possible that these professional communicators may interpret events in ways that do not take the public's values into account and may recommend policies contrary to those values.

Still another possible problem is that media organizations themselves—perhaps motivated by owners' political points of view, or by long-range profit maximizing that seeks happy advertisers and friendly government policies, not just contented readers and viewers—may try to advance their own political agendas. Perhaps they slant news stories, or air apparently diverse but actually self-serving sets of commentary. Such efforts would be particularly worrisome if carried out by leading media outlets (e.g., elite newspapers) that may be able to influence other media and shape public debate.

These concerns suggest many questions about mediated deliberation, some of which we can address here.

QUESTIONS ABOUT MEDIATED DELIBERATION

From the perspective of democratic theory, those who deliberate in or through the media should be acting for (representing) ordinary citizens. In order to assess how well they do so, we need to know a number of things about who speaks and what they say. Are the speakers and viewpoints diverse? Are voices heard from every corner of society? Or are professional communicators unrepresentative of the public in important ways? If so, does the public have any recourse, any way to break through a monolithic media consensus in order to inform and express itself?

Do the media present high-quality, relevant, diverse ideas and expertise? What about public officials? Do they sometimes dominate the media with narrow sets of ideas and preferences, limiting the competition of ideas?

Do media organizations themselves play active parts in deliberation, pursuing their own policy objectives? If so, do they use subtle techniques that may deceive unwary readers and viewers? Do some media outlets have sufficient influence over other media that they can affect the course of public deliberation for the country as a whole?

Plan of the Book. This book cannot hope to provide definitive answers to these questions, but the following chapters attempt to illuminate some of them by drawing upon three case studies of mediated deliberation. Each case study takes a close, intensive look at a small but important example of deliberation in the mass media. Two of them involve scrutinizing dozens of different media outlets, examining news and opinion pieces in many different newspapers, magazines, and television programs, in order to present rather full pictures of nearly everything important that was said in the major media about their particular topics. A third case focuses on a special, elite forum for political deliberation, the editorial and op-ed pages of the *New York Times*.[35]

The cases all come from the United States in the early 1990s. This restriction in time and space limits the generality of conclusions that can be drawn, since individual professional communicators, media outlets, and technologies all vary from country to country and change rapidly over time. Some broad patterns in mediated deliberation that these cases reveal, however, may be widespread and persistent. In any case, unity of time and place has advantages for continuity, coherence, and thoroughness of analysis. As successive snapshots of recent incidents in U.S. political history, the cases (which are arranged in chronological order) also illustrate some of the political forces involved in that history, in the rise and fall of the Bush presidency and the early troubles of the Clinton administration.

Chapter 2 deals with the autumn 1990 debate, in the editorial and op-ed pages of the *New York Times,* concerning whether or not to go to war with Iraq. This chapter indicates that even an apparently open and vigorous media debate can be *constructed* so as to serve the editorial purposes of a media organization, and it suggests that certain elite newspapers like the *Times* may play leading parts in shaping the character of national debate.

Chapter 3, concerning the charge that "1960s programs" were responsible for the 1992 riots in Los Angeles, illustrates a number of general points about mediated deliberation, including the great speed with which ideas can be exchanged, the predominant role of public officials and other professional communicators, the distinctive editorial stands taken by various media outlets, the ways in which editorial viewpoints can correspond with slants in news stories, and the leading political roles sometimes played by certain elite newspapers.

Chapter 4, on the 1993 nomination of Zoe Baird to be U.S. attorney general, indicates that the mainstream media and the bulk of public officials and other professional communicators sometimes do (for class-related or other reasons) get out of touch with ordinary citizens, but that—at least under certain limited circumstances—alternative communications channels like talk radio can facilitate popular uprisings that seize back control of debate.

Chapter 5 offers some general observations about these

cases and relates them to other evidence concerning how well mediated deliberation does or does not serve democracy in the contemporary United States.

NOTES

1. Dahl (1989, 111–12, 181–82) specifies "enlightened understanding" (adequate and equal opportunities for each citizen to learn what would be in her or his best interest) as one criterion for a democratic process.

2. Interests are here defined in terms of the preferences a citizen would hold if she or he were well informed about the consequences of alternative policies. This is close to the positions of Dahl, Connolly, Rawls, Sidgwick, and others; see Dahl (1989, 180–81, 307–8).

3. The kind of democracy I advocate, involving strict majority rule, is what Robert Dahl (1956) once labeled "populistic democracy." It is opposed by various advocates of "pluralistic democracy," who favor special responsiveness to intense or well-organized groups, and by those in the tradition of Schumpeter (1950), who define democracy in limited procedural terms, such as the presence of competitive elections for leaders. For a broader procedural approach, see Dahl (1989). For arguments pro and con majority rule (including a discussion of May's Theorem), see Dahl's chapter 10.

Absent strongly overlapping cleavages in society (which could lead to majority tyranny), I believe that majority rule ought to prevail, subject only to protection of fundamental rights—especially political rights. The attractiveness of majority rule also depends crucially, however, upon effective public deliberation.

4. For evidence on this "rationality" of the public, see Page and Shapiro (1992, esp. chap. 10).

5. This simple definition of deliberation, as reasoning and discussion about the merits of public policy, is widely used in the literature (see notes below). But it fuzzes over a number of issues concerning precisely what deliberation is and what it does: whether it simply involves exchanges of information about the consequences of alternative policies, for example, or whether it entails fundamental changes in individuals' preferences or values. See McCubbins and Lupia (1995); Austen-Smith (1990).

6. See Dewey (1954 [1927], 176–84).

7. On frank speech in ancient Athens, see Monoson (1994, 1996).

8. On the public sphere and its early manifestations, see Habermas (1989 [1962]; 1992, esp. 446, 449–50), Herbst (1993), and Calhoun (1992).

As Peters (1993) points out, Habermas has been ambivalent about the media, seeing them as having liberating potential but advocating norms of equal participation that are rooted in (and, I would say, only realizable in) face-to-face, small-group situations.

9. On town meetings, see Mansbridge (1980), Bryan (1995).

10. Discussions of legislative deliberation include Federalist no. 63, in Hamilton, Madison, and Jay (1961 [1787–88], 382–90), J. S. Mill (1958 [1891]), Bessette (1978, 1994), Muir (1982), Maass (1983), Derthick and Quirk (1985), Kelman (1987).

11. I see Fishkin's (1991) small-random-sample "deliberative opinion polls" as useful, in certain low-information situations, for ascertaining how a well-informed public would (will?) react to a particular candidate or policy. But such polls are potentially dangerous: who decides exactly what information is to be provided to the sample? (If none, little is gained over ordinary discussions among members of the public.) In any case, deliberative polls are not satisfactory substitutes for deliberative public opinion among the citizenry as a whole, for only the citizenry as a whole can be entrusted with controlling its representatives.

A suggestion that would preserve the virtues of egalitarian, face-to-face deliberation among a small, representative group of citizens, but would help enlighten the public as a whole rather than substituting for it, is to carry out regular, nationally televised "representative town meetings," in which small samples of randomly chosen citizens question experts and public officials and debate public policy among themselves, for the benefit of their fellow citizens. The Kettering National Issues Forums, among others, have this potential. On the related idea of "citizen juries," see Crosby (1995). Boyte (1995) urges going beyond deliberation to encourage action, public work.

12. Barber (1984, esp. 173–98), argues for "political talk" as central to strong democracy. I favor as much vigorous, local deliberation as possible, so long as citizens are also linked together into a deliberative national public so that all have access to the same (and the best) information and ideas. For better or worse, only mass media can provide such a linkage.

13. Even in smaller collectivities like Athenian Assemblies or New England town meetings, time has generally been too scarce for everyone to talk. Already some division of labor and representation occurs informally; the hope (enforced, to a degree, by social norms) is that only those with something important to say and some minimal skill at saying it will speak up. The need for division of labor is much magnified in a huge collectivity like a modern nation, and specialization is more institutionalized as a result.

14. A classic—though outrageously elitist—argument for representative government is Mill (1958 [1861]).

The perennial problem of how to ensure that legislators properly represent their constituents has an analogue in the central problem addressed here: how to ensure representativeness by professional communicators.

15. Dewey (1954 [1927], 176, 184).

16. Garnham (1992, esp. 364–67) neatly outlines both the inevitability of mediated deliberation and some major normative questions that mediation raises.

17. For discussions of certain types of high-visibility professional communicators, see Soley (1992), Alterman (1992), and Reese, Grant, and Danielian (1994).

18. Bagdikian (1992, 18–26) calculates that, at the beginning of the 1990s, twenty-three large corporations dominated all types of major media. They did half or more of the business in each main field—newspapers, magazines, television, book publishing, and motion picture production.

19. Bennett (1988, esp. chap. 2) discusses the fragmented, dramatized, and personalized nature of television news.

20. On the role of cues and cue givers in opinion formation, see Sniderman, Brody, and Tetlock (1991) and Ferejohn and Kuklinski (1990).

21. The fact that deliberation is largely mediated does not mean that citizens play no part in it or that (as in the old "injection" model of media effects) they merely absorb what is transmitted. They pick and choose, talk and think. For evidence that audiences actively process and discuss political information, see Graber (1984) and Gamson (1992). Gamson emphasizes that audiences use experiential knowledge and popular wisdom (including adversarial "counterthemes") as well as media discourse, and that they often integrate material from the different sources.

22. Page and Shapiro (1992, esp. chap. 2, 10), discuss how collective deliberation can be successful in a mediated setting despite low information levels among the citizenry.

23. Garment (1991), Sabato (1991), Jamieson (1992), and Patterson (1993) trenchantly analyze media-transmitted scandals, negativity, and dirty politics.

24. Arguments that the media have a liberal bias are given in Braestrup (1976) and Lichter, Rothman, and Lichter (1986), but Entman (1989, chap. 2) refutes them with considerable success.

25. Evidence of a conservative bias can be found in Parenti (1993) and Gitlin (1980).

26. On nationalistic, pro-official biases in media reporting on foreign policy, see Hallin (1986), Dorman and Farhang (1987), Herman

and Chomsky (1988), Bennett (1990), and Page and Shapiro (1992, chaps. 5–6, 9).

27. Difficulties with the concepts of bias and objectivity are discussed in McQuail (1992, esp. 183–95).

28. On the beneficial effects of competition among ideas, see J. S. Mill (1947 [1859]), Holmes (1919), Zaller (1992, 310–32), Page and Shapiro (1992, 15–27, 362–66); and, for a formal rational-expectations model, McKelvey and Ordeshook (1986). Various concepts of media diversity are discussed in McQuail (1992, 141–81).

29. Several examples of sensible collective policy preferences formed in the face of propaganda or falsehoods are given in Page and Shapiro (1992, chaps. 3–6).

30. Various ways in which the marketplace of ideas can fail are discussed in Page and Shapiro (1992, 394–97), Ferguson (1995, esp. appendix), and Entman and Wildman (1992).

31. The potency of officials as news sources is thoroughly demonstrated in Sigal (1973), Gans (1980), and Hallin (1986). The role of officials and former officials in op-ed commentary will be addressed in chapter 2.

32. These examples of official control and distortion of political information are discussed in Goulden (1969, on Tonkin), Gervasi (1986, on Soviet missiles), Marchetti and Marks (1984, on covert operations), and Ford (1984, on nuclear energy).

33. Downs (1957) and Davis, Hinich, and Ordeshook (1970) discuss conditions under which electoral competition may push two parties toward the position of the median voter.

34. On the power of money (that is, major political investors, working through the two-party system) over policies and ideas, see Ferguson (1995), Ferguson and Rogers (1986).

35. Specialists in communication studies will see that much of the novelty of the findings reported here results from the research design. Few scholars have previously studied editorial and op-ed pages as forums for political deliberation, or explored the possibility of editorial construction of public debate, as chapter 2 does. Equally uncommon in the literature are multimedia analyses, like those of chapters 3 and 4, covering practically everything said in the major media about specific policy issues. I believe that only such comprehensive case studies can begin to reveal the anatomy of mediated deliberation, in which ideas fly about from one television program, newspaper, or magazine to another.

TWO

The New York Times
Goes to War with Iraq

Since public deliberation concerning policy issues is now largely carried out through the mass media, by professional communicators, there is good reason to look closely at forums within which the most prominent and influential communicators interact with each other and speak to broader audiences. One such forum is the editorial and op-ed pages of the *New York Times*.[1]

The *Times*, particularly on issues of foreign policy, is one of the most prestigious and authoritative publications in the United States.[2] It is read by foreign-policy decision makers and experts,[3] as well as by the editors, reporters, and commentators who decide what will appear in other mass media. Thus the opinions voiced in the *Times* also tend to find their way—directly, or through syndication, or by trickle-down processes involving editors, writers, and commentators in other media—to a mass audience. The quality of deliberation in such a forum could affect the quality of debate generally.

It is appropriate to assess whether or not the voices and views presented in such a key forum live up to the normative standards we associate with democratic deliberation. To what extent are the authors and viewpoints presented on the editorial and op-ed pages of the *Times* diverse? Are they balanced? Do they include the most pertinent ideas, the best available expertise, and all major points of view? Are they representative of the American citizenry as a whole?

Open Debate. There are some reasons to expect substantial diversity and openness, even a miniature "public sphere,"[4] in the editorial and op-ed pages of the *Times*, especially on crucial questions like whether or not the United States should go to war.   17

The *Times* is taken very seriously by its readers, and the *Times,* in turn, takes its central position in policy debates very much to heart. It invites anyone, unsolicited, to submit an opinion column or a letter to the editor, and it spreads publication opportunities widely to many letter writers and guest columnists. Embracing ideals of responsible journalism, the *Times* apparently feels an obligation to publish not only all news, but also all opinions that are "fit to print." The chief editor of letters to the editor, for example, wrote in his 1990 guidelines that publication of a letter indicated the *Times* felt a position should be presented, not that it was the position of the paper; his major aim was a "balanced forum." He claimed that letters to the editor continued to be "the most democratic forum in the world."[5]

One might expect, therefore, that in a major debate like the lengthy and intense discussion in autumn 1990 concerning war or peace with Iraq, the *Times'* editorial pages would present a wide range of voices, including representatives of ordinary working people (perhaps union leaders), leaders of religious and ethnic organizations (particularly Jewish, Muslim, and Arab groups), members of civil-rights, peace, and women's groups; people concerned with "peace dividends" and domestic spending, proponents of international law and collective peacekeeping, advocates of military strength, people concerned with access to Middle Eastern oil, and many others. Particularly given some scholars' assessments that the formation of foreign policy is now substantially democratic,[6] one might expect the *Times'* editorial and op-ed pages to conduct a free-wheeling debate in which ordinary citizens would have a voice, many ideas would contend, and a variety of policy options would be discussed.

Official Sources. On the other hand, there are reasons to be skeptical of any such expectations. For one thing, many studies tell us that news stories in the *New York Times* and other mass media tend to be heavily dominated by official sources plus a small set of experts, and there is some evidence that the same thing is true of commentary and opinion.[7] This is particularly the case with respect to foreign affairs, where relevant information is often hard to obtain and is largely, sometimes exclusively, held by governments.[8] We might expect that in op-ed debates the authoritative voices of officials and former officials would be featured, along with some nongovernmental experts—especially those enjoying legitimacy by virtue of positions at leading universities and think tanks. Still, opinion columns and letters to the editor might constitute a more free forum than news stories, since the editorial pages are less hurried, less dependent upon cultivating official sources for daily information handouts, and less restricted to reporting on standard beats; they might be more open to a variety of voices.

Another set of reasons to doubt the open-forum model of editorial and op-ed pages, however, concerns the nature of editorial objectives and processes.

A Theory of Constructed Deliberation. Major U.S. newspapers, obviously, are not town meetings or village squares: they are mostly private, for-profit businesses, owned by large corporations or (like the *Times*) closely held by families. In either case—but perhaps especially in the case of family ownership, where a newspaper or a chain of papers may be viewed as an instrument for personal expression rather than just a tool for making money—newspaper owners and managers have partisan loyalties and policy preferences that may tend to be reflected in their publications' editorials and endorsements of political candidates, and may tend to creep into news coverage as well.[9] It would be surprising if owners' and managers' values and preferences had no effect upon the overall shape of what they printed on their editorial and op-ed pages.

The opportunities for control are extensive. Newspapers' own unsigned editorials, of course, can be expected to reflect the views of editors and, to varying degrees, of the owners who appoint editors and in some cases stay in touch with them. In addition, regular opinion columnists need not simply represent diverse views from society at large; columnists can be hired, retained, promoted, and encouraged so as to further owners' and editors' aims.[10] Guest columns can be accepted or solicited at the editors' pleasure. Many would-be columns come in "over the transom," of which only a few are selected; some columns are actively sought out by the editors; and still others are negotiated and reshaped after inquiries by potential authors.

Even the apparently free discourse in letters to the editor can be controlled by accepting (or perhaps soliciting) mainly those letters that are congenial to editorial purposes. Major national publications get floods of letters; the *Times*, for example, received some 350–400 letters to the editor *per day* in the early 1990s.[11] Newspapers can decide for themselves, on any basis they like, which letters to print. The *Times* ordinarily prints 7 or 8 letters per day, fewer than 3 percent of those received.[12]

It would be too much to expect that such opportunities for control of the editorial and op-ed pages would be entirely neglected. On the contrary, one would anticipate that, at least under certain circumstances (e.g, when dealing extensively with policy questions they care a lot about), editors at the *Times* and elsewhere may consciously or unconsciously *construct* a public debate. They may speak in a somewhat coordinated fashion through unsigned editorials and regular opinion columns and may print carefully selected guest columns and letters to the editor, in such a way as to advance their own policy views. Such constructed deliberation could convey an impression of diverse participation and vigorous debate, while actually tending to lead readers in predetermined directions congruent with editorial policy. Indeed, the very appearance of vigorous debate could make the editors' views more persuasive to readers than they would otherwise be.

DATA ON THE *TIMES'* EDITORIAL PAGES AND IRAQ

The notion of constructed deliberation is a rather general one, applicable to many media under many circumstances. It meets a fairly hard test in a case like that of the *New York Times,* which has pretensions to openness, and in connection with a major issue like the debate leading up to the Persian Gulf War, about which millions of Americans had strong opinions and for which there was abundant time to gather and publish a wide range of views. If deliberation were constructed by this newspaper in this case, there would be reason to suspect that the phenomenon is widespread.

The present chapter will focus on the crucial second phase of the confrontation with Iraq, which lasted from November 9, 1990, through January 15, 1991. After Iraq's August 2, 1990, invasion of Kuwait, President Bush declared that the invasion "will not stand"; he sent thousands of American troops to Saudi Arabia, assembled an international coalition against Iraq, and persuaded the United Nations Security Council to impose strict economic sanctions that banned practically all trade with Iraq unless and until it would withdraw from Kuwait. The tight sanctions, the troop buildup (which reached about 150,000 men and women by early autumn), and the commitment to defend Saudi Arabia enjoyed wide support in the United States. On November 8, however, just after the 1990 congressional elections, Bush announced that he had begun a further buildup (which eventually doubled U.S. forces in the region), in order to ensure an adequate "offensive capability" that could be used against Iraq. Bush's announcement provoked the first serious elite dissent from administration policy and led to extensive public discussion of whether or not the United States should go to war. After the offensive buildup was complete, and after both the UN Security Council and the U.S. Congress had authorized the use of force (contingent upon the exhaustion of diplomatic efforts), the United States-led coalition on January 16, 1991, launched a month-long air attack and then a four-day ground blitz that pushed Iraqi forces out of Kuwait and destroyed much of Iraq's infrastructure. President Bush's popularity soared.[13]

Our concern is with the two-month-long November-to-January debate over whether and when to use military force. During this period, the *New York Times* editorial and op-ed pages devoted a great deal of attention to the Iraq issue. A computerized search found 144 columns and editorials and fifty-three letters to the editor—a total of 197 pieces—that mentioned Iraq. Since some of these alluded to Iraq only in passing (or dealt with peripheral matters or did not extensively discuss future U.S. policy), for certain purposes we will concentrate on the approximately one-half of them that offered reasonably serious and sustained discussions of key aspects of U.S. policy. For other purposes the whole data set will be used. Reference will also be made to news coverage during this period and to some earlier editorial material that helps provide context.[14]

WHOSE VOICES WERE HEARD

Readers of the *Times'* editorial and op-ed pages between November 1990 and January 1991 may well have been impressed with the apparent diversity of the nearly 200 editorials, columns, and letters to the editor concerning Iraq. The scores of different au-

Table 1
Authors of Discussions of Iraq in *New York Times* Editorial Pages, Nov. 9, 1990 to Jan. 15, 1991

| | Editorials and Columns | | | | Letters to Editor | |
| | All Mentions | | Significant Discussions | | | |
Author	n	%	n	%	n	%
Editors of *NYT*	32	22.2	20	25.6	0	0.0
Regular *NYT* columists	63	43.8	34	43.6	0	0.0
Officials or former officials	13	9.0	8	10.3	5	9.4
Academics	12	8.3	7	9.0	10	18.9
Affiliates of think tanks	10	6.9	6	7.7	1	1.9
Writers	10	6.9	3	3.8	0	0.0
Policy advocates	2	1.4	0	0.0	5	9.4
Businesspersons or professionals	2	1.4	0	0.0	4	7.5
Labor representatives	0	0.0	0	0.0	0	0.0
"Ordinary" citizens	0	0.0	0	0.0	28	52.8
Total	144		78		53	

thors seemed to represent a variety of backgrounds and ideological tendencies.

But much of this diversity was an illusion. In the first place, a very large part of the discussion of Iraq was carried on by editors and regular columnists employed by the *Times* itself. As table 1 indicates, two-thirds (66 percent) of the 144 columns and editorials mentioning Iraq (69 percent of those that extensively discussed policy) were written by the editors or by regular columnists. The columns were about twice as frequent as the editorials.

The thirty-two unsigned editorials concerning Iraq, which appeared on the average just about every other day of our sixty-eight-day period, clearly represented a major editorial engagement with the Iraq issue. The editors cared about it and worked hard to make their views known. Such a high level of engagement suggests (though, of course, it does not prove) that motivation may have existed to shape the rest of the editorial and op-ed pages in a fashion congenial to the editors' own stands.

The regular opinion columnists also seemed deeply concerned about Iraq: they collectively came up with a comment on the subject just about once every day, on the average, during this period. William Safire, the most intensely focused, wrote fifteen columns dealing with Iraq; Anthony Lewis wrote twelve; Tom Wicker, ten; A. M. Rosenthal, eight; Flora Lewis, six; Anna Quindlen, four; James Reston, three; Leslie Gelb (whose column began only in January), three; and Russell Baker, two, for a total of sixty-three. The fact that various combinations of these nine different names tended to appear on different days may have helped give casual readers of the *Times* more of an impression of diversity than was warranted by their repeated appearances or by the similarities in what they said.

To be sure, the regular columnists' viewpoints were by no means identical; some (especially Safire and Lewis) disagreed sharply with each other. As we will see below, however, the range of expressed disagreement was not actually very wide, and the center of gravity of the regular columnists' views corresponded closely with the editorial position of the *Times*.

Much of the apparent diversity in the *Times'* op-ed pages was produced by the forty-nine Iraq-related guest columns, written by nonemployees of the *Times*, which ran under many different bylines. But here, too, the impression of diversity was somewhat misleading, because the vast majority of these column writers occupied positions in mainstream institutions and organizations associated with the foreign-policy establishment.

About one-quarter of them (thirteen) were public officials or former public officials.[15] These included former presidents Jimmy Carter and Richard Nixon, Senators Bill Bradley, Sam Nunn, and Jim Sasser, former secretary of defense Casper Weinberger, and former secretary of state Alexander Haig. Another fairly large group consisted of twelve academics, mostly from universities near New York, Washington, or Boston (Princeton, Columbia, New York University, City College of New York, Georgetown, George Washington, Harvard, Massachusetts Institute of Technology, Boston University), and many with government ties.[16] Nearly as many (ten, some of them also academics) were coded as journalists or writers, whom the *Times* identified as authors of relevant works (e.g., Richard Rhodes on nuclear weaponry, Gary Hufbauer and Kimberly Elliott on economic sanctions) or general literary figures (Germaine Greer, Donald Dewey). And another ten guest columnists were affiliated with think tanks: the Council on Foreign Relations (three), the Brookings Institution, the Center for Strategic and International Studies, the International Institute for Strategic Studies, and a scattering of others.

This was, without question, an impressive set of guest columnists, with some interesting things to say. Yet what is most striking, in retrospect, is not the luster of the names that appeared but their establishmentarian character. Many important categories of citizens and thinkers were represented sparsely or not at all.

Curiously, for example, experts on the Middle East, as opposed to general strategic or military analysts, were not very prominent in the *Times'* deliberations about Iraq. True, Judith Kipper, Rashid Khalidi, Nadav Safran, and Edward Said did appear, but Kipper's qualifications are not unassailable,[17] and Khalidi, Safran, and Said were printed only at the last moment (after December 25), barely before the United States went to war. Beyond those four, the *Times'* op-ed page presented very few experts on what was happening within the Arab world, on past U.S.-Iraq relations, on the nature and merits of past disputes between Iraq and Kuwait, or—most strangely—on Iraq itself. This gap seems explicable only by the fact that the *Times'* own editorial stand (as manifested in its unsigned editorials, which are discussed below) disagreed in important respects with the views of most students of Iraq and the Arab world. Furthermore, only a small scattering of voices clearly representing Arab, Israeli, Jewish, or Muslim points of view was heard: just Edward Said (a member of the Palestine National Council), a Jordanian television host, an anonymous "Kuwaiti businessman," and Edgar Bronfman of the World Jewish Congress. No voices appeared from Iraq's democratic opposition, which opposed war. None came from Iraq, period.

Other important categories of people were altogether absent from the *Times'* opinion columns. It is not surprising, perhaps, that no ordinary, uncredentialed citizens were granted access to such a prestigious and demanding means of expression as a *New York Times* column; division of labor may preclude that particular kind of source diversity or representativeness. But religious leaders and moral philosophers, who at various periods in American history have played major roles in debating military and foreign policy, were not represented at all.[18] Similarly, not a word appeared from the leaders or rank and file of organized labor, who had much at stake if the United States was to go to war. Equally conspicuous was the lack of voices from peace organizations or civil-rights or women's groups. And, of course, there were virtually no radicals—no communists, socialists, libertarians, anarchists, pacifists, or others outside the *Times'* conception of the mainstream.

To be sure, some of these absences may have been voluntary, rather than resulting from selective or exclusionary practices by the *Times.* Parts of the peace movement, for example, fell silent because of the repellent nature of Hussein's behavior, concern about Israel, and/or perceptions that war was unlikely. But other dissenters did their best to be quite vocal.[19] The absence of dissenting voices in the *Times* was so nearly total as to make a wholly voluntary explanation quite implausible.

In the opinion columns of the *New York Times,* then, the voices deliberating about war with Iraq failed to be very diverse or representative. In addition, certain kinds of expertise and a number of important, relevant voices were missing.

Letters to the editor, presumably a more spontaneous and populistic mode of expression, might be expected to rectify some of these lacks. To some extent they did. About one-half of the fifty-three published Iraq-related letters came, as best one can tell, from ordinary citizens,[20] adding a measure of grass-roots input to the editorial and op-ed pages' otherwise rather elite cast of characters. (See table 1.) Moreover, a handful of letters appeared from the kinds of advocacy organizations that were mostly shut out of columns: SANE/Freeze, World Citizen Diplomats, and the Fund for Free Expression.

Still, these letters hardly transformed the *Times'* editorial pages into an open, free-wheeling, grassroots debate about policy toward Iraq. In the first place, there were not many letters. The total of fifty-three letters to the editor was far outweighed by the 144 editorials and columns; it averaged out to fewer than one letter per day during the sixty-eight-day period. (This was not simply a matter of lack of space; only about one-seventh of all the letters published by the *Times* during this period dealt with Iraq.) Moreover, as is generally the case, most letters were much shorter and less conspicuous than a column; only the occasional symposium, in which three or four letters appeared under a common headline, could match the visual impact of one editorial or opinion column.

Furthermore, although half the letters were written by ordinary citizens, the authors of the other half bore occupational or institutional affiliations closely resembling those of the mainstream establishment column writers. Ten letters came from academics, more than half of whom were affiliated with Columbia University (e.g., Roger Hilsman, Hans Smit, Demetrios Caraley, Charles Black), and one came from a think tank. Five were written by officials or former officials, including a member of the army reserve, a sergeant in Saudi Arabia, a retired Foreign Service officer, and an intelligence analyst. Four came from business or professional people, some of whom seemed to be peddling their own wares (an international legal consultant, the publisher of an oil industry newsletter, the actuary of a life insurance fund, a lawyer).[21] The five letters from political-advocacy groups were a drop in the bucket.

As with the columnists, very few letter writers offered comprehensive expertise on Iraq or the Middle East. Arab, Israeli, Jewish, and Muslim organizations were represented only by one letter from the executive director of the American Jewish Congress. The letters, like the columns, were entirely devoid of any identified spokespersons for labor, women, or civil-rights groups.

WHAT THEY SAID

Perhaps the most compelling evidence of constructed deliberation comes from the fact that the entire assemblage of the *Times'* editorials, op-ed columns, and letters to the editor about Iraq formed a coherent whole, which is best understood in terms of the editors' own policy preferences (as stated in their unsigned editorials). That is to say, while the viewpoints expressed on the editorial and op-ed pages were by no means uniform, they fit together in such a way as to advance the *Times'* editorial position, and few of them departed very far from it.

The *Times'* editorial stand on Iraq was clear and consistent;

it did not change much from the early days after Iraq's invasion of Kuwait until the onset of the air war. From the beginning, the *Times'* unsigned editorials condemned the Iraqi invasion and insisted upon a complete and unconditional withdrawal from Kuwait. They opposed offering any concessions to Iraq on such matters as a port on the gulf (which had been excluded from Iraq by British boundary-drawing), oil fields on the Iraq-Kuwait border (where the Kuwaitis were alleged to be stealing Iraqi oil by slant drilling), oil prices (which Kuwait had depressed, to Iraq's detriment, by producing much more than its OPEC quota), past aid to Iraq for fighting Iran (for which Kuwait demanded repayment in full), or—of particular concern to the *Times*—international talks about Palestinian independence from Israel. Iraq's repeated offers to withdraw from Kuwait in return for concessions on such points were ignored or flatly dismissed.[22]

The *Times'* editorials supported President Bush's commitment of U.S. troops to Saudi Arabia for defensive purposes and favored Bush's and the UN's impositions of strict economic sanctions that cut off virtually all of Iraq's trade with the world. They expressed alarm, however, at the post-November 8 U.S. buildup of offensive capability and advocated patience: the sanctions were doing their job; Iraq would eventually be forced to withdraw from Kuwait. The United States should stay steadfast with sanctions and avoid premature use of military force.

This position put the *Times* on the dovish side of the U.S. policy debate, but its opposition to war was limited and contingent. The *Times'* editorials indicated that war might eventually be necessary; they simply wanted to give sanctions time to work and opposed any hasty or premature use of force.[23] (Indeed, once the war began, the *Times* quickly climbed aboard.) Moreover, in prewar criticisms of Bush administration policy the *Times'* editorials devoted little attention to the horrors of war or to possible terms for negotiating a peaceful solution. Instead they focused on procedural matters, urging Bush to better "explain," or "articulate," or "give reasons" for his policies, insisting that Congress be consulted, urging that there be public "debate" about Iraq, and counseling "patience." Such procedural objections, however reasonable and potentially important they may have been, ultimately proved feeble in the face of alarms about

Iraqi nuclear weapons, doubts about the cost and feasibility of keeping U.S. troops in Saudi Arabia and holding the alliance together for an extended period, and the eventual congressional approval of using force.

In its first major editorial on Iraq after President Bush announced the offensive troop buildup, for example ("Too Far Too Fast in the Gulf," Nov. 11), the *Times* opposed this "unilateral declaration of offense." Iraqi aggression could not be allowed to stand, but the solution was sanctions, congressional and U.N. involvement, and open debate. "Desert Sword: Time for Answers" (Nov. 14) called for Congress to be heard and for the administration to articulate its policy, as did the biting "Double Insult from the President" (Nov. 16), which rejected Bush's criticisms of dissent by Senators Lugar (R-Ind.) and Moynihan (D-N.Y.). (The *Times* seems particularly comfortable editorializing within a rubric of bipartisanship.) "A Weak Case for War in the Gulf" (Dec. 2) tried to refute various administration arguments for its abrupt shift to the offensive. "Who Can Declare War" (Dec. 15) and "War by Default" (Dec. 16) asserted that only Congress had the authority; it should debate and vote.

Many editorials (e.g., Nov. 18, 25, 29, Dec. 1, 7, 21) asserted that sanctions were working and asked "what's the rush?" to use force. At the same time, "Israel and Iraq, Unlinked" (Dec. 19) opposed any UN connecting of Palestinian issues with Kuwait. "No Booty for Iraq. None" (Dec. 24) expressed opposition to any compromises ("dirty deals") that would leave Iraq with gains from the invasion; this hard line was only slightly modified in "How to Bargain with a Blackmailer" (Jan. 5), which called for the complete and unconditional departure of Iraq from Kuwait but alluded vaguely to the possibility of accommodations after withdrawal, in accord with "sensible" and long-standing U.S. policies. "Iraq's Untenable Argument" (Jan. 11) again rejected linkage of other Middle East issues to a Kuwait solution.

"Where Is Congress on the Gulf?" (Jan. 3) called yet again for Congress to debate and vote. ("Congress's Calhoun Strategy" [Jan. 7] likened Congress to a football player who refused to carry the ball.) "The Larger Patriotism" (Jan. 10) said it would be wise for Congress to vote no on authorizing force, but after Congress's yes vote, "The Message, Stronger" (Jan. 13) rationalized that it had sent a clear message to Iraq to get out of

Kuwait; a continued embargo and peaceful solution was still preferred. This editorial continued, however, to oppose any last-minute compromise on oil or the islands.

Several of the *Times'* regular op-ed page columnists took stands quite close to those of the unsigned editorials, sometimes using similar or identical language. This was true, for example, of Tom Wicker (Nov. 14, Dec. 2, 30, Jan. 2), of James Reston (Nov. 13, Jan. 2), and of Leslie Gelb (Jan. 2, 6, 13). Gelb, in "A Final Pause" (Jan. 13), said Bush should pause for some weeks to let the congressional message sink in and should fashion an Arab fig leaf for Iraqi withdrawal from Kuwait; let Israel propose Mideast peace talks after withdrawal. These regulars were supported, in various ways, by a broad array of guest columnists: Bill Bradley (Nov. 15), Judith Kipper (Nov. 16), John Judis (Nov. 20), Peter Tarnoff (Nov. 29), Casper Weinberger (Dec. 2), Rami Khouri (Dec. 15), Arthur Schlesinger Jr. (Dec. 17), Ann Lewis (Dec. 20), Nadav Safran (Dec. 27), Doug Bandow (Jan. 3), Theodore Sorenson (Jan. 10), Richard Ullman (Jan. 12), and Gary Hufbauer and Kimberly Elliott (Jan. 14).

Other regular columnists arrayed themselves a bit to the dovish side or a bit to the hawkish side of the *Times'* editorials. Anthony Lewis was, in relative terms, the most insistent dove. On November 12, shortly after President Bush's announcement of the offensive buildup, Lewis correctly analyzed "The Logic of War": by adding troops and calling off the troop rotation plan, Bush had made a commitment. If Hussein did not withdraw from Kuwait by early 1991, Bush intended to use military force. In subsequent columns Lewis deplored the "ghastly" consequences of war. Besides often echoing (in some cases anticipating) the editorials' calls for public debate and for the involvement of Congress, Lewis advocated a negotiated settlement (e.g., Nov. 23, Dec. 10): perhaps just a face-saving agreement not to attack if Hussein would withdraw and return the hostages (Dec. 3); perhaps a diplomatic arrangement for withdrawal, followed by arms limitations in the Middle East (Dec. 14); perhaps including new initiatives for Arab-Israeli peace—even continued Iraqi control of oil fields and gulf islands might not justify war (Dec. 31); perhaps an "Arab solution" and an international peace conference (Jan. 11).

Lewis's calls for negotiations with Iraq put him in a very

small minority, at the extreme dovish end of the *Times'* op-ed continuum. Yet Lewis's dovishness had distinct limits. He, like the unsigned editorials, rejected "linkage" of the Palestinian problem with Kuwait; he made clear that the conquest of Kuwait had to be reversed; he spoke of possible use of force as a last resort. As Lewis's subsequent hard line on Bosnia illustrates, "tough Tony" (Safire's phrase) is no pacifist.

More than half of the relatively dovish op-ed pieces on Iraq came from Lewis. He was supported, to varying degrees, by a few columns from regulars Anna Quindlen (Nov. 25, Jan. 13), James Reston (Nov. 30), and Tom Wicker (Dec. 5), and by guest columnists Richard Rhodes (Nov. 27), David Shipler (Dec. 22), Rashid Khalidi (who offered a comprehensive outline for a negotiated solution, Dec. 26), Jimmy Carter (proposing a U.S.- and Soviet-sponsored conference on the Israeli-Palestinian question, Jan. 2), and Roger Morris (also with concrete suggestions for compromise, Jan. 9).[24]

Somewhat to the hawkish side of the unsigned editorials were numerous op-ed columns by regulars William Safire and A. M. Rosenthal, supported in whole or part by a handful of guest columnists: Alton Frye (Nov. 11), Andrew Bennett (Nov. 11), Alexander Haig (Dec. 10), Richard Nixon (Jan. 6), and Edward Luttwak (Jan. 13.) Most of these columnists emphasized the danger that Iraq would use missiles and weapons of mass destruction—chemical, biological, or nuclear—on its neighbors. They generally advocated early military action to wipe out Iraq's capabilities and insisted not only on unconditional withdrawal from Kuwait, without compromise, but also on war crimes trials and Iraqi payment of reparations.

The sharp-penned Safire led this faction. Offering authoritative-sounding specific details about "yellowcake," "gas centrifuges," and the like—which he claimed to have got from "world spookery" (presumably meaning U.S. and Israeli intelligence)—Safire repeatedly warned that Iraq was rapidly developing nuclear weapons (Nov. 12, 19, 26, 29, Dec. 27). If Mario Cuomo's ideas for a negotiated settlement were to prevail, Safire ominously suggested, Cuomo as president would have to fight a nuclear war (Nov. 26). Safire wanted to "take out" Iraqi nuclear, chemical, and biological weapons installations with heavy air strikes, followed, if there were no withdrawal from Kuwait, by a massive invasion of ground forces (Nov. 29, Dec. 13, Jan. 7, 10).

Rosenthal, too, called for eliminating Iraqi missiles and chemical and nuclear weapons (Nov. 13, Dec. 11) and ruled out any negotiated compromise (Dec. 11, Jan. 11); he differed from Safire chiefly in stressing the need for democracy in the Middle East and in more explicitly emphasizing dangers to Israel rather than to the United States.[25] Guest columnist Frye advocated seizing a chunk of western Iraq, if it came to war (Nov. 11); Bennett called for attrition by air attacks (Nov. 11); Haig pushed the Munich analogy (Dec. 10); Nixon argued for eliminating Iraq's capacities (Jan. 6); and Luttwak advocated massive air strikes (Jan. 13).

Taken together, these relatively hawkish and dovish opinion columns flanked the *Times'* unsigned editorials, on both sides, in a remarkably symmetrical and well-balanced fashion. A total of eighty-one editorials and opinion columns could be categorized as falling into one or another of the three groups characterized above: the dovish columns that advocated a peaceful solution (presumably involving negotiated concessions, though few spelled this out); the editorials and columns that favored an extended trial of sanctions but then force, if necessary, to ensure complete and unconditional Iraqi withdrawal from Kuwait; and the hawkish columns that advocated the early use of military force to destroy Iraq's military capabilities and drive Iraqi troops out of Kuwait. As table 2 indicates, half the coded pieces— 49 percent of them, including all eighteen unsigned editorials plus twenty-two opinion columns—took the "middle ground," sanctions-first position. (This already high figure is probably somewhat understated, since rather small deviations from the editorial middle ground were categorized as hawkish or dovish.) One-quarter (26 percent) of the pieces, twenty-one opinion columns, took a dovish, antiwar—and, in a few cases, pronegotiations—stand. And an almost exactly balanced one-quarter (25 percent) of the pieces, twenty columns, took a hawkish, attack-soon position.

Whether intentionally or unintentionally, then, consciously or unconsciously, the editors of the *Times* employed, solicited, and selected op-ed columnists and columns in such a way as to

Table 2
Policy Views on Iraq in *New York Times* Editorial Pages,
Nov. 9, 1990 to Jan. 15, 1991

	Pursue Peaceful Solution		Use Sanctions First, Force If Needed		Use Force Soon		
	n	%	*n*	%	*n*	%	Total
Editorials	0	0.0	18	100.0	0	0.0	18
Opinion columns	21	33.3	22	34.9	20	31.7	63
Total	21	25.9	40	49.4	20	24.7	81
Letters to editor	10	66.7	4	26.7	1	6.7	15

construct a distribution of views in which their own editorial position ended up exactly in the center, with all the persuasive advantages of centrist-seeming positions in our pluralistic, compromise-oriented society.[26] By judicious choice of opinion columns, the center of the distribution could presumably have been made to come out almost anywhere. (This illustrates one of the problems with balance as a normative standard. It is not easy to specify exactly which views deserve full presentation—there are usually more than two sides to a question—or to specify what midpoint they should be balanced around.)

To be sure, there are possible explanations for the *Times'* op-ed lineup other than its construction for political purposes: an unbiased sampling of views submitted to the *Times*, for example, or a market-driven desire to please a generally centrist audience. The substantial divergence between the *Times'* stand and the views of average Americans (see below), however, casts grave doubt upon the latter possibility. The former is also implausible, particularly since the *Times* is known to solicit columns rather than waiting passively for over-the-transom submissions, but no data are available to test it systematically: we cannot know how many or what sort of potential columns the *Times* ignored or rejected.

The distribution of *Times* editorial and op-ed views was not democratically representative in the sense of reflecting citizens' preferences. A set of pieces that mirrored the views of ordinary Americans, as measured by opinion surveys, would have tilted much more toward compromise and negotiation. Surveys reported in the *Times* and elsewhere showed that "compromise" was much more popular than war (Nov. 1990), and that large majorities (79 percent on Jan. 9, 1991, 64 percent on Jan. 13) favored additional talks with Iraq before President Bush's January 15 deadline; smaller majorities (53 percent, 57 percent) favored more talks *after* the deadline, a possibility barely hinted at in the *Times*. Most Americans resisted territorial concessions to Iraq unless the Kuwaitis agreed, and large majorities opposed a deal in which Israel would give up the West Bank and the Gaza strip in return for Iraq's giving up Kuwait. But a majority of the U.S. public preferred making concessions on the disputed oil fields rather than using military force (Dec. 1990), and large majorities (66 percent on Jan. 9, 67 percent on Jan. 13) favored an international conference on Arab-Israeli problems if that got Iraq to withdraw from Kuwait without war.[27] Several of these options, endorsed by large numbers—even majorities—of Americans, were barely mentioned in the editorial pages of the *Times*.

Not only did the center of gravity of views on the *Times'* op-ed page match the *Times'* own editorial stand and differ from the predominant opinions of ordinary Americans, the *range* of views displayed was also narrow. It largely "indexed" the range of official debate, in just the way that some scholars postulate that news stories do.[28] Unlike the case of news coverage, however, where indexing may result from news-gathering routines designed to elicit quick, regular, authoritative news stories under pressures of haste and competition, adherence to a narrow set of views on the op-ed page, at least in sustained cases like this one, is clearly voluntary. Before the Gulf War began, the *Times* had many weeks in which to gather and print as broad a diversity of views as it wished. But the editors chose to present a restricted set of official, mainstream opinions not deviating much from their own stand.[29]

In condemning the Iraq regime's aggressiveness and malevolence, the *Times* sometimes came close to echoing President Bush's overblown comparison of Hussein with Hitler.[30] There was little attention to Kuwait's provocations (oil price cutting, slant drilling, refusal to negotiate), or to governments elsewhere—including the United States recently in Panama—that had enjoyed armed conquests with impunity, or to Iraq's internal social and economic accomplishments, or authoritarianism and inequality in Kuwait and Saudi Arabia, or the existence of nuclear and mass-destructive weapons in other dirty hands around the world. There was certainly no talk of U.S. imperialism or hegemony, or of our historical policy of trying to control Middle Eastern oil resources. In assessing the possible costs and benefits of war there was some discussion of possible U.S. casualties, but virtually none about the likely fate of Kurdish and Shiite teenagers who had been conscripted into Hussein's army, or the probable damage to Iraqi civilians—especially the elderly and children. (After the war, it was estimated that some forty-nine thousand Iraqi children died from malnutrition and disease attributable to the destruction of Iraq's infrastructure, an effect that Jack Geiger refers to as "Bomb Now, Die Later.")[31] The sensitive topics of controlling oil and protecting Israel as motives for war were hardly touched.

In terms of the ideas presented in the *Times'* editorials and opinion columns, then, deliberation was seriously defective. It did not meet standards of content diversity, presentation of all major points of view, democratic representativeness, or the communication of relevant facts and expertise.

Nor does consideration of letters to the editor do much to change this conclusion. True, the published letters did not just echo the columns and editorials; they tended to be much more dovish and to express more concern about the death and devastation of war, including effects on Iraqis. Roger Hilsman's (Nov. 27) and Hans Smit's (Nov. 27) letters, for example, offered detailed arguments for a negotiated settlement, as did Charles Black's (Jan. 2). Black wrote, under the headline "Do We Want to Be the Butchers of Baghdad?" about the dreadful fate that would befall the Iraqi people under a massive bombardment. Of the fifteen letters that could be categorized, ten—two-thirds of them—favored substantive negotiations, while just four favored something like the *Times'* sanctions-first stand, and only one advocated the early use of force.[32]

These letters extended the range of debate and tilted the

editorial pages a bit away from perfect symmetry around the *Times'* editorial position. But their small numbers, together with their short length and inconspicuousness, limited the effect. Ten dovish letters over a sixty-eight-day period of debating war and peace did not amount to a lot.[33]

Most published letters to the editor did not take a clear stand on the major policy questions concerning Iraq; instead, they dealt with side issues, some of considerable importance (the president's war powers, the legal force of UN resolutions, the military draft), but many of less crucial significance: the size of the population of Kurdistan, reinstatement of the Reserve Officers Training Corps, letter writing to soldiers in the gulf, foreign workers in Kuwait, insurance exclusions of war damages, Saudi women drivers, Japanese attitudes about Gulf War costs and the U.S. "Jewish lobby," censorship in Saudi Arabia, the legalities of occupation versus annexation, the Eisenhower Doctrine, and the like. While several of these letters were interesting and informative, they played only a peripheral part in deliberations about war or peace.

CONCLUSION

To casual readers, the editorial and op-ed pages of the *New York Times* in the autumn of 1990 appeared to be full of vigorous debate over whether or not the United States should go to war with Iraq. A multitude of editorials, columns, and letters to the editor seemed to offer a variety of views, often in an interesting and intelligent fashion. They debated the issues in a manner suggestive of a miniature public space, or public sphere, of democratic deliberation.

Yet the open and democratic character of this debate was partly an illusion. The diversity of voices and views offered (that is, both source and content diversity) was limited. Although there was indeed "balance" (rather precise balance) among three sets of policy stands, other major viewpoints were not included. Ordinary citizens' opinions were not well represented, in the sense that some widely held views were not presented in proportion to their adherents among the general public—or, indeed, presented much at all. Certain kinds of highly relevant expertise were given little or no hearing.

Most of the voices speaking on the editorial and op-ed pages were those of the *Times'* editors, regular columnists employed by the *Times*, or guest columnists holding mainstream positions in officialdom or academia. Few ordinary citizens—and virtually no radicals, pacifists, or other outsiders—were heard; organized labor and religious, peace, women's, and civil-rights groups were largely absent. Experts on Iraq or the Arab world were rare.

The viewpoints expressed on the editorial and op-ed pages generally mirrored official debates. They covered a rather narrow band of opinion, ranging from a few that advocated negotiations with (and mild concessions to) Iraq, through many that upheld continued economic sanctions, to some that advocated the early use of military force. Nearly all accepted the goal of forcing Iraq entirely out of Kuwait. None at all took Iraq's side; none argued that the United States and United Nations had no business to intervene. Contrary to widespread preferences among the American citizenry, very few pieces proposed serious negotiations. Moreover, the columns were arranged, in a balanced and symmetrical fashion, so that they flanked—on the hawkish and the mildly dovish sides—numerous "centrist" editorials and columns that called for continued sanctions, and force if necessary later, to bring about complete Iraqi capitulation. (A few letters to the editor added a slight and not very conspicuous dovish input.)

The narrow range of views expressed, and the symmetry with which they fell on both sides of the *Times'* editorial stand, indicate that deliberation about Iraq was consciously or unconsciously *constructed* by the *Times* editors, with the effect of advancing their own policy views. This lineup resulted from voluntary editorial choices, largely free of day-to-day newsgathering pressures; *Times* editors had many weeks in which to gather and print whatever views they wished.

How important were the editorial and op-ed views presented by the *Times*, in the context of the nationwide debate about war or peace with Iraq? In theory, at least, many other voices might have spoken through other media channels, and attentive citizens could have judged which made most sense. But the centrality of the *Times* as a source of foreign-policy information and interpretations for policymakers and opinion leaders suggests that it may have had a substantial impact upon what was heard elsewhere. The limitations of debate in the *Times* were in fact matched in many or most other print and electronic media.[34]

Of course, we cannot be sure that other media were influenced by the *Times;* they may have engaged in their own, independent but similar constructions of debate, drawing their definitions of legitimate policy alternatives from a relatively narrow foreign-policy elite rather than from broader groups in society or from ordinary citizens. If so, they did it by choice: news-gathering reasons (reliance upon easily reached news sources for quick, repeated information handouts) would not be sufficient to explain the media's voluntary self-limitation to the same narrow elites, over a lengthy period, in their commentary and opinion columns. In either case—leadership by the *Times* or independent but similar choices by other media—the result was a constricted public debate about war with Iraq.

The indications of constructed deliberation at the *Times,* a highly prestigious publication that purports to conduct a democratic and free-wheeling debate on its editorial and op-ed pages, suggests that such practices may be quite widespread. Lesser publications are presumably even less inhibited from constructing their editorials, opinion columns, and letters so as to support their editorial positions.

This examination of editorial and op-ed pages suggests, then, that under certain conditions, certain media outlets may not serve as neutral, passive transmitters of societal ideas and interpretations, but may take an active part as articulators of policy views. (In the following chapter, we will examine another case in which several elite newspapers apparently did so, using news stories as well as editorials and opinion columns.) To the extent that leading media outlets can shape the debate in other media—or other media speak with the same voice for reasons of their own—and to the extent that the media truncate debate or advance viewpoints that conflict with those of ordinary citizens, democratic deliberation may suffer.

NOTES

1. The *Times* editorial page, made up of unsigned editorials and letters to the editor, faces the op-ed page (with signed regular and guest opinion columns), at the back of the first section of the paper. Visually

and functionally they form a unit; for convenience, they will sometimes be referred to collectively as *editorial pages* or as the pages containing *editorial material,* to distinguish them from news pages.

2. In 1995 (according to an advertisement in the *Columbia Journalism Review,* Jan.–Feb. 1995, 2) the *New York Times,* for the second year in a row, won the Gold Award for the Best Op-Ed Page.

3. On the importance of the *Times* to foreign-policy decision makers, see Cohen (1963). See also Powlick (1990), for officials' use of news media to ascertain "public opinion."

4. On the public sphere, see Habermas (1989 [1962]), Calhoun (1992).

5. R. A. Barzilay memo, "Letters to the Editor," September 19, 1990. I thank Mr. Barzilay for providing his memo and for discussing the letters columns in a telephone interview, October 27, 1994.

6. Russett (1990) and Deese (1994) analyze the role in U.S. foreign-policy making of public opinion and democratic processes generally.

7. Sigal (1973) and Gans (1980), among others, document the importance of officials and experts as news sources. Soley (1992) and Reese, Grant, and Danielian (1994) extend the finding to certain kinds of media commentary.

8. On the central role of officials in dominating foreign-policy information that appears in the media, see Hallin (1986), Bennett (1990), and Herman and Chomsky (1988).

9. The controversial issue of ownership influence on news content will be addressed in the next chapter. Here we are concerned solely with the *Times'* editorial and op-ed pages, where *a priori* doubts about owners' influence (based upon norms of journalistic independence and the like) would seem to be much less plausible.

One might conjecture that the editorial stands of corporate-owned newspapers would often be subordinated to profit-making considerations and would tend to reflect the revenue-related concerns of the newspapers themselves or of other corporate holdings. (Such concerns could, of course, include highly political matters like labor relations, taxes, and government regulation.) Thus the editorial stands of corporate-owned media may closely follow an industrial-sector pattern, whereas family-owned media, like the *Times,* may sometimes give more free rein to the personal ideologies and idiosyncrasies of owners. On the other hand, some corporate chieftains like Hearst and Murdoch (on Murdoch, see Shawcross 1992, e.g., 144–45) have also had distinctive ideologies and idiosyncrasies that may have been reflected on the editorial pages of their publications.

10. At the *Times,* such influence is probably exerted largely or exclusively through the hiring and retention of columnists, not through

overt intervention in what they write. In a letter to this author (May 31, 1994), Anthony Lewis stated that in twenty-five years as a columnist he never had any suggestion of what line he should take, on the conflict with Iraq, Vietnam, the Middle East, or a dozen other controversial matters.

11. Interview, R. A. Barzilay, October 27, 1994. The number of letters submitted to the *Times* has subsequently risen to some *500* per day (telephone conversations with "Annie" and "Janet" of the *Times'* letters department, Oct. 25, 1994).

12. Another illustration of the great discretion that publications can wield over their letters columns is *Time* magazine's comment, after the 1992 Los Angeles riots (June 1, 1992, 15), that they received 425 letters on the subject. By my count they printed only 18, 4 percent of those received.

Given the tiny fraction of submitted letters that the *New York Times* prints, it generally shies away from publishing multiple letters from any one individual. A notable exception may hint at some of the *Times'* principles of selection: the all-time champion letter writer (with more than 50 letters to the editor published by the *Times* since 1949) appears to be Jimmy Warburg, renegade liberal scion of the prominent banking family (Chernow 1993, 580).

13. A thorough history of the Gulf War and the buildup to it is given in Freedman and Karsh (1993).

14. On news coverage during the prewar debate, see Entman and Page (1994).

15. The figure in table 1 of thirteen officials, constituting 26.5 percent of the forty-nine guest columnists, understates their numbers a bit. At least two of those identified as academics (Roger Hilsman and Arthur Schlesinger Jr.) had also held public office. The categories used here are not mutually exclusive; in fact, they all tend to intermingle. Columnists' positions were coded on the basis on the affiliation first mentioned by the Times.

One employee of a political party (Ann Lewis) and a former hostage (Thomas Ewald) were included as officials.

16. One guest columnist classified as academic was a graduate student at Southern Illinois University; the rest were faculty members.

17. Kipper's graduate degree was in clinical psychology; she did not know Arabic or Hebrew and had had little or no experience in the Middle East. See Cumings (1994, 107).

18. Andrew Rojecki (1994) has shown that the voices of U.S. religious leaders in media-reported arms control debates faded markedly between the 1950s and the 1980s.

19. On the many opponents of war who were largely ignored in the

Times and other media, see Sifry and Cerf (1991) and N. Chomsky (1992).

20. The best available indicator of "ordinary citizen" status is the simple absence of any identification of occupation or affiliation. At times, however, this may exaggerate citizens' ordinariness, as when Corliss Lamont, the wealthy philanthropist and activist, was not identified as such—either by his own signature or by one of the Times' capsule descriptions—in his letter of December 24. The *Times* ordinarily does not print titles or descriptions when it considers them irrelevant to the subject under discussion (Barzilay memo, Sept. 19, 1990).

21. None of these, however, was so blatant in self-promotion as Gerald Bennerts, president of American Hydrolines, whom the Times allowed (in a Nov. 13 letter, just before our period of study) to make a pitch for the U.S. Navy to buy his speedy hydrofoil boats.

22. On Iraq's offers to withdraw from Kuwait in return for various concessions, which were rejected by the U.S. government and dismissed or ignored by the *Times* and other media, see N. Chomsky (1992, 190–93, 203–10), and Kellner (1992, esp. chap. 1).

23. After the war, two editorial employees of the *Times* separately indicated in my presence that the editors actually opposed the use of force against Iraq under virtually any circumstances. But the editorials that were printed certainly did not say so. Perhaps the editors calculated that more "moderate" appeals, including their emphasis on procedural issues, would be more effective. If so, they may have been mistaken.

24. Tom Ferguson's powerful antiwar column on the "Five Horsemen of the Apocalypse" appeared after the period studied and in the Business section of the *Times* (Feb. 3, 1991, sec. 3, 13), so it is not included in this analysis of the editorial and op-ed pages.

25. Concern about Israel was clearly central to Safire and Rosenthal, who had begun a drumbeat against Saddam Hussein well before the invasion of Kuwait, after Hussein threatened to "scorch" Israel if Israel were to repeat its 1981 attack against Iraqi nuclear facilities. See Freedman and Karsh (1993, 32–33), and Alterman (1992, chap. 12). It may have been an important motivation for *Times* owners and editors as well, although the editorials rarely mentioned Israel.

26. I have no direct evidence on exactly how and why the construction of the *Times'* editorial and op-ed pages came about—whether or not it was conscious, for example, and whether it arose from consideration of policy views or from a more general conception of which voices are legitimate in the discussion of foreign policy. But certain hypotheses, such as market-driven audience pleasing, or random sampling of submitted columns, are doubtful or clearly false (see the text, below), so that the selection of columns very likely manifested a source- or con-

tent-related *choice* by editors (possibly reflecting the values of the owners and publisher who in turn hired those editors). Most important are the fact of harmony between editorial and op-ed stands, and the likelihood that it resulted from source- or policy-related choices.

The question of causal mechanisms will arise again in the following chapters, when we address connections between news content and editorial stands and the possible roles therein of owners and editors.

27. Mueller (1994, 36–37, 231, 237–41). Mueller's book includes a full compendium of survey data on public attitudes about the gulf crisis and war.

28. Bennett (1990) discusses the mainstream media's tendency to index debates among public officials, that is, to provide a guide to the range of officials' positions, rather than go beyond them.

29. We can only speculate about why editors at the *Times* and elsewhere often stick close to public officials in their commentary as well as news stories: perhaps for effective participation in elite policy debates; perhaps to further their own editorial stands, which tend to be close to the official center.

30. On the frequent media repetition of the Hussein-Hitler analogy, and its genesis in preinvasion criticism of Saddam Hussein by A. M. Rosenthal, Moshe Arens, and others, see Dorman and Livingston (1994, 69–75).

31. Geiger (1994), describes the postwar public-health disaster in Iraq.

32. It is impossible to tell whether the printed letters to the editor were representative of the much larger number of letters received, because those received but not printed have not been preserved. Barzilay indicates that letters supporting the *Times'* own editorial policy were generally disfavored ("rarely used," Sept. 19, 1990, memo); he looked for a "balance of opinion" between "*the* [emphasis added] pro and con of any particular debate" (interview, Oct. 27, 1994). A tendency to favor letters disagreeing with the *Times'* editorial stands suggests a safety valve function for published letters: in this case, perhaps, a safety valve needed because many *Times* readers were more dovish on Iraq than the newspaper was.

My investigation of letters to the editor has convinced me that the assumption by some historians, that published letters in old newspapers are a representative sampling of public opinion, may be quite erroneous.

33. On November 8, just before the period of this study, an additional three letters under the headline "No, We Don't Have to Go to War with Iraq" argued strongly against Daniel Pipes's call for war (Oct. 23) and against an editorial's inflexibility about negotiations (Oct. 21). To add them to the analysis would not change the conclusions.

34. Evidence of limited debate on Iraq in other media outlets as well as the *Times* is given in Carroll (1991), Bennett and Paletz (1994), Kellner (1992), Chomsky (1992), and Cumings (1992, chap. 4).

This uniformity across media could reflect influence by the *Times* in helping set the parameters of debate, or could—perhaps more plausibly—indicate that virtually all mainstream U.S. media constructed the terms of debate (either for policy- or source-related reasons) in an independent but quite similar fashion. (Again, any such construction represented editorial choices, largely free of daily newsgathering constraints.) Either way, the narrowing of debate had important implications for democratic deliberation.

THREE

Assigning Blame for the Los Angeles Riots

In this chapter we look beyond the op-ed world of the *Times* to a case of deliberation that played out through news stories, as well as editorials and commentary, in a wide range of media—newspapers, magazines, and television programs.

After the April 29, 1992, acquittal on state charges of five police officers accused of beating Rodney King, three days of bloody and destructive riots broke out in south central Los Angeles.[1] Shortly thereafter, the chief spokesman for the Bush White House suggested that an important cause of the riots had been liberal social programs of the 1960s and 1970s. That charge was quickly and overwhelmingly rejected by most public figures quoted in the mass media, by most media editorials and commentaries, and by most members of the general public.

Such a very brief and bounded case of public deliberation is susceptible to a particularly thorough sort of investigation, covering a wide range of different media, which is not feasible for broader issues (like war with Iraq) debated over many weeks or months. This case illustrates what appear to be several general patterns in mediated deliberation, including the remarkable speed with which debate can occur, the predominant role of officials and other professional communicators, the distinctive editorial stands taken by various media outlets (especially newspapers), the ways in which editorial viewpoints tend to creep into news stories, and the leading roles sometimes played by elite newspapers like the *Wall Street Journal,* the *New York Times,* and the *Washington Post.* This case also illustrates some conditions under which presidential communications efforts can fail and helps illuminate the drastic decline in President Bush's popularity from its Iraq war high to the low that preceded his 1992 election defeat.

A computer search of the Nexis database and a manual search of university library stacks and microfilms were used to obtain texts or transcripts of all news stories and commentaries concerning the "1960s programs" charge, for one week after the charge was made (a period that included most media activity), in a wide variety of print media and television programs. Several television networks, sixteen newspapers, and eleven magazines were examined.[2]

This search turned up many scores of stories and programs, of which 129 were directly relevant. Not all U.S. media were covered, of course—that would not be possible even for so quick and finite a case as this one. But a very broad range of media was examined, and (because of redundancy among media outlets) those studied are likely to have included most of the material that appeared elsewhere. Most U.S. media outlets focus on the same news sources; television news and local papers rely heavily on the Associated Press and *New York Times* news services; many interpretive columns are syndicated; and officials and pundits migrate from one television channel to another, repeating the same messages. Any important idea or statement tends to show up in many different places. It is unlikely, therefore, that we missed much of relevance in the major, mainstream media.

CHARGE: LIBERAL SOCIAL-WELFARE PROGRAMS DID IT

At the end of April 1992, as television news shows broadcast images of burning buildings, looting, and assaults in Los Angeles, a few partisan interpretations of the riots began to be offered, but they initially received little media attention. On Thursday morning, April 30, front-running Democratic presidential candidate Bill Clinton briefly criticized President Bush's rather austere initial reaction ("the court system has worked"; what's needed now is calm and respect for the law), commenting that the violence had been worsened by "more than a decade of urban decay" caused by lowered federal spending in the cities. But after White House spokesman Marlin Fitzwater criticized "Slippery Bill" for playing politics when cities were burning and people were being killed, Clinton fell silent. This skirmish got little television or newspaper coverage. Nor was there much coverage of AFL-CIO president Lane Kirkland's comment that the riots were symptomatic of a decade of favoring the rich and privileged while ignoring and injuring the disadvantaged, or House majority leader Richard Gephardt's reference to "twelve years of neglect," or similar comments by Democratic National Committee chairman Ron Brown and Texas governor Ann Richards.

A *Wall Street Journal* editorial on Friday morning, May 1, argued against "another flood of federal guilt money" into institutions and ideas that had "already failed." NBC evening news that day showed Arthur Fletcher, chairman of the U.S. Civil Rights Commission, calling for leadership like Lyndon Johnson's; it recapped highlights of the War on Poverty and then showed President Bush at the University of Michigan the previous year criticizing Johnson's programs as well-intentioned but backfiring, creating dependency and weakening moral responsibility. On CNN's *Crossfire,* cohost and former Bush chief of staff John Sununu suggested that programs of the 1960s generally did nothing but produce an "unconscionable dependence on welfare." (Cohost Michael Kinsley countered, "Millions of people have been taken out of poverty.")

Although none of these remarks got much attention, they helped lay the groundwork for the later "1960s programs" flap. So did Clinton's somewhat more publicized criticism, on Saturday, May 2, of the Republicans' Willie Horton campaign and the vice president's "divisive" attacks on welfare, and similar remarks by Representative Maxine Waters (D-Calif.) and Ron Brown that made the *CBS Evening News.* CNN aired some sharply conservative opinions about related matters. On *Capital Gang,* Robert Novak declared that "the system we have had of welfare, spending billions and billions of dollars, is a terrible system." When Mark Shields suggested that the Great Society could not be responsible for the prevalence of single parents in inner cities, because it had ended twenty-four years ago, Mona Charen left him sputtering: the Great Society had been "reinforced" ever since, she said, even by Ronald Reagan, Richard Nixon, and Jerry Ford. On CNN's *Both Sides with Jesse Jackson,* Pat Buchanan, Bush's right-wing Republican challenger, clearly stated the argument that the administration later adopted: "after the Watts riots we launched the Great Society," and "the

American taxpayers contributed hundreds of billions of dollars and more than a trillion dollars. . . .We saw the results, I think, in south Los Angeles—the utter, rank failure of the welfare state, in south Los Angeles."

Similarly, on Sunday, May 3, on ABC's *This Week with David Brinkley,* Attorney General William Barr (perhaps launching a trial balloon, but not attracting much notice) said that we were seeing in inner cities "the grim harvest of the Great Society," because welfare policies contributed to family breakdown. Jack Kemp, the secretary of Housing and Urban Development, whom the riots had just brought out of policy exile, told a television audience that Clinton had "stooped to partisan demagoguery" by accusing the Republicans of helping to cause the violence.

Real media attention and full-scale debate, however, came only on Monday, May 4, when the Bush administration tried to take the political offensive. Echoing Buchanan and Barr, the White House attacked social programs associated with the Democrats as causes of the riots.

Immediately after a cabinet meeting, presidential spokesman Fitzwater called a press briefing. Garbling his lines a bit, he declared, "We believe that many of the root problems that have resulted in inner-city difficulties were started in the '60s and '70s and that they have failed." "[W]e're now paying a price" for the failures of social-welfare policies. Those programs ignored the relationship between people's pride in a community and having a job, property, and a stake in the community. Programs that "redistribute the wealth" or involve "direct handouts" "we believe are wrong." Fitzwater contended that liberal Democrats in Congress had prevented Bush and Reagan from winning changes in welfare policies and social programs that might have helped avert the disturbances. Acknowledging that "[t]his is a political year," he said the administration was trying to show "what our direction is" by starkly contrasting "destructive" social programs supported by past Democratic Congresses with Bush's conservative agenda that "creates jobs and housing and home ownership and involvement in a community."[3]

Presidents and their spokespersons are prime sources of news, often getting media attention. The evening news shows on all major television networks, a few minutes into "aftermath" or "back to normal" stories about Los Angeles, turned to political implications and quoted or clipped Fitzwater. CNN reported snippets of Fitzwater's comments on a series of news and discussion programs. Newspaper headlines the next morning (Tuesday, May 5) announced, "White House Links Riots to Welfare" (*New York Times,* p. A1); "White House Blames Liberal Programs for Unrest" (*Washington Post,* p. A8); or "Bush Blames '60s Programs; White House Tries to Link L.A. Riots, Democrats' Policies" (*Chicago Tribune,* p. A1).

RESPONSE: "NONSENSE"

Negative reactions to Fitzwater's remarks came quickly, however. At the press conference itself reporters seemed skeptical; when they repeatedly pressed Fitzwater to give specific examples of the social programs he had in mind, he replied, "I don't have a list with me."

On the evening of the press conference (Monday, May 4), ABC news, after giving a few seconds to Fitzwater's comments, devoted a long, eight-minute segment to an "American Agenda" story on urban poverty that (while undoubtedly scheduled earlier) seemed to rebut Fitzwater by emphasizing negative effects of Reagan-Bush era cuts in federal programs: sociologist William Wilson called the federal response to urban problems "pathetic," and Jonathan Kozol said filthy school buildings signal society's contempt for inner-city kids. PBS's *MacNeil-Lehrer* showed Democratic presidential candidate Jerry Brown saying Fitzwater was totally wrong; Jack Kemp gave a reluctant-sounding partial defense of Fitzwater ("I don't want to spend my time . . . ") and was roughed up by five big-city mayors, who spoke of "decades of neglect" of the cities and maintained that programs like block grants and CETA public jobs had worked well until they were eliminated by the Reagan administration.

Further illustrating the amazing speed with which deliberation can proceed through electronic media, CNN aired several brief discussions of Fitzwater's comments the same day he made them. On *Moneyline,* Jack Kemp conceded to Lou Dobbs, "I don't know that I would say it the same way"; Fitzwater was reacting to the "terrible attack" on the president by Clinton and Ron Brown. On *Crossfire,* Michael Kinsley asked the ubiquitous Kemp why, when the Great Society programs had been passed twenty or thirty years before and were subsequently cut, the riot was happening now. He asked exactly which Great Society programs Fitzwater was talking about; Kemp said he would name two programs that trapped people in poverty: public housing (where rent "jumps" up if a tenant gets married) and Aid to Families with Dependent Children (AFDC) (which "punishes" people who form a family and "subsidizes" a family that breaks up). But after Kinsley asserted that the real value of welfare had plummeted, so that family breakup should be less of a problem now, not more, Kemp backed off a bit: "I wouldn't say that the welfare system per se causes it, but it certainly accommodates it and allows it to happen." Only conservative economist Walter Williams, on *Larry King Live,* said he largely agreed with Fitzwater.

The next morning (Tuesday, May 5), the *New York Times*—as it may often do—helped define the parameters of political debate for other media and for the country, both by raising the salience of Fitzwater's remarks (through a page 1, middle-of-the-page news story just above the fold, plus an editorial), and by framing critical interpretations of them.[4] In the news story, Michael Wines summarized Fitzwater's charge and added that the White House refused to say whether the president would offer any detailed alternatives to those "failed" policies in coming weeks. Wines asserted that the spokesman had acknowledged that "the main thrust of the White House response was political." The story also quoted Fitzwater's "don't have a list" reply and said that Fitzwater's remarks placed the issue "squarely in an election year political context," only days after Fitzwater had berated Clinton for playing politics with the riots. The story commented that many social programs, especially the most expensive and comprehensive ones, had become "part of the fabric of American life": yearly increases were expected in Social Security, Medicare, Medicaid, aid to schools, food stamps. And it declared that even Bush's advisers agreed privately that conservative alternatives had received only "tepid" support from the president. Each of these critical themes played a significant part in the subsequent public debate.

The *Washington Post* initially placed its news story less prominently than the *Times* (p. 8 instead of p. 1), but it offered a similarly critical interpretation. Ann Devroy, like Wines, simultaneously reported Fitzwater's charge and undermined it, noting the pledge of new activism for conservative solutions proposed "but rarely pushed" by President Bush. Like Wines, Devroy interwove discrediting material through the story, commenting, for example, that the White House criticism came "as" (because?) a new poll showed Bush losing his election lead and locked in a three-way tie with Clinton and Perot. She also quoted an unnamed Republican official's deflating remark that the campaign against liberal solutions "would work a little better if we were running against a Great Society liberal" instead of Clinton. She noted that Fitzwater had refused to name any specific program. And she judged that, in the year since Bush's speech at the University of Michigan about "failed" Great Society programs, there had been "no evidence of a comprehensive new policy."

Perhaps surprisingly, the rather conservative *Chicago Tribune*'s page 1 story by Timothy McNulty included discrediting material much like that in the *Times* and *Post*. It used a political frame—that White House officials had tried to "pre-empt criticism" of Reagan-Bush social policies by blaming failed liberal programs "of earlier decades"—and took note of Fitzwater's refusal to cite specifics. The *Tribune* then quoted Clinton's response that Fitzwater's remarks were "the last refuge of a desperate person" and that the Republicans in 1981 had abolished the programs Fitzwater was attacking. The article went on to comment that administration leaders were "still defensive"; an official said the attack had been decided upon after Bush aides watched weekend talk shows that emphasized the president's lack of a domestic agenda.

Other newspapers reported Fitzwater's remarks along with varying amounts of criticism but confined most of the criticism to quoted reactions. The *Los Angeles Times* (May 5, p. 9) employed a rather deadpan reporting style, just noting Fitzwater's failure to cite any specific "studies" or programs and quoting California Assembly Speaker Willie Brown (D-S.F.), who responded that the president was "disconnected from reality" and "flat wrong." Similarly, the *Atlanta Constitution* (p. 14) commented that the administration's "finger-pointing drew criticism from all sides," quoting only Democratic National Committee official James Desler, who said the administration was "really stretching it" this time. The *Miami Herald* (p. 1), also mostly deadpan, quoted Boston's Democratic mayor Ray Flynn (head of the U.S.

Conference of Mayors) as saying that Fitzwater's philosophy was "inconsistent with American values and principles." The *St. Louis Post-Dispatch* (p. 1) reported Fitzwater's comments in a neutral fashion but included, fairly high up in the story, Clinton's rebuttal that the Republicans kept running against liberal programs that they had pummeled out of existence. Even the *Wall Street Journal's* news story (p. 3) commented that Bush was "still groping" for a response to the riots and that, despite the White House focus on liberal-versus-conservative solutions, Clinton's ideas included elements that "some Bush officials" (such as Kemp) and other conservatives also favored.

In two key newspapers, the *New York Times* and the *Washington Post,* editorials and opinion columns chimed in on the same day (Tuesday) as their first news stories. The *Times* editorialized that it would be "silly and wrong" for Bush to continue Fitzwater's line, which was a "pinched, ideological" response to a national tragedy. Many Great Society programs had been consistently successful, for example, Head Start and the Job Corps. The *Washington Post* ran an even tougher and longer editorial rebuttal. The White House had sent out Fitzwater to create a "historical caricature." Given the choice between a calm and substantive or a tinny response, the president "unerringly chose tin" and distorted the events of the past week. After quoting Fitzwater at length, the *Post* alluded to cuts during the last twelve years in programs involving housing, jobs, and community involvement, precisely the areas Fitzwater claimed to favor. The theory had been that everyone would gain if only government would get out of the way. "It did and they didn't." The dark side of Reagan's morning in America had been a huge increase in income inequality and poverty. Federal aid to the cities and minorities was cut. The Bush administration had been coasting; Kemp was isolated, and even he did not have a full urban program. Now, with the Los Angeles upheaval, the administration was just hunkering down and considering political implications.

Clearly the interpretive material in the news stories run by the *Times* and *Post* tended to be in tune with their editorial policies.[5] This could happen (and, in my observation, it often does happen) without breaching the *Times'* proudly proclaimed "wall of separation" (noncontact) between the news and editorial departments, for the simple reason that owners and publishers ultimately control both; they have the power to hire and fire. It is hardly surprising that editors and reporters with views congenial to owners tend to be hired, encouraged, and promoted, or that those with deviant inclinations tend to adapt or depart.[6]

Opinion columns have a more complicated relationship with newspapers' editorial policies. Most papers want to *seem*, at least, to display diverse viewpoints. Still, newspapers generally control their editorial and op-ed pages with care. In the *Times* and the *Post,* for example, the center of gravity of op-ed opinions offered, the central tendency of views displayed, often bears a striking similarity to the overt editorial stands of the paper (recall the Iraq war example in the previous chapter).

On Tuesday morning, the same day as the first "1960s programs" news story and editorial, regular *New York Times* columnist A. M. Rosenthal briefly remarked that there was "no time" to argue either with leftist doomsayers or with administration apologists who said liberal poverty programs were all to blame; people needed jobs and relief from violence. In her front-section (p. A2) column in the *Post,* Mary McGrory sarcastically wrote that the suspense was over concerning how Bush would respond to the riots: he had sent Fitzwater out to finger the scapegoats. She hoped for "presidential majesty," not partisan recriminations. Regular *Post* op-ed columnist Richard Cohen (without explicit reference to Fitzwater's charge) offered a scathing indictment of George Bush as proven "insufficient for the presidency," asserting that the cities had been told to "shove off" for twelve years. Bush's domestic policy had been "stupid and inattentive"; Bush had expressed no outrage at the verdicts, had shamelessly used a civil-rights bill for political advantage, and had scapegoated welfare without proposing any sort of solution.

Later that day (still Tuesday, May 5), Bill Clinton alluded to the morning's newspaper headlines and told the American Newspaper Publishers convention, "It's just amazing"; "Republicans have had the White House for 20 of the last 24 years, and they have to go all the way back to the '60s to find somebody to blame. . . .I was appalled." He attributed the riots in part to "twelve years of denial and neglect" of festering social problems under Presidents Reagan and Bush.

The phlegmatic Fitzwater, besieged by reporters, asserted

that he had been "misunderstood"; he had not meant to imply that Great Society programs caused the riots. An anonymous high official (Fitzwater? Kemp?) called reporters together to say that social spending had actually *grown* under Bush.

Tuesday evening's news programs on CBS and NBC (but not ABC) featured "political fallout" from the riots, including clips of Clinton responding to Fitzwater. NBC also ran a clip of Vice President Dan Quayle saying that Great Society thinking hadn't worked. CNN again aired several conservative comments, by Republican strategist Mike Murphy—who came under heavy crossfire from Michael Kinsley and former representative Tony Coelho (D-Calif.)—and by the Cato Institute's Edward Crane, among others, but on *Larry King Live*, Secretary of Labor Lynn Martin went no further than to say that some programs "haven't worked very well." Even former Reagan cabinet official William Bennett, on the same program, conceded, "I don't think it helps much to say . . . Great Society programs were the problem." CNN news headlined, "President Bush Ridiculed for Passing the L.A. Buck"; Catherine Crier said Fitzwater's suggestion had been called ridiculous "by those who should know," including some Republicans and political analysts and many poor Americans. She declared that "many [unnamed] analysts" said the Great Society was never fully funded because the Vietnam War siphoned off resources and Republican administrations began dismantling what was left. (Guest William Bennett demurred: "I mean, something like $2 trillion later, an awful lot of money has gone in," but he did not link it to the riots.)

On Wednesday morning, May 6, newspapers prominently— and, for the most part, approvingly—reported Clinton's response to Fitzwater. Robert Pear, for example (*New York Times*, p. 1), under a headline stating that Clinton had tied the riots to "Neglect" and "'12 Years of Denial' under Reagan and Bush," noted the "paradox" of the Republican attack when liberals had criticized Clinton for abandoning liberal programs and when he was trying to steer a middle course similar to Kemp's on domestic policy. Pear also mentioned that Bush was letting his own proposals "languish." An inside-page *Times* story by David E. Rosenbaum (p. 24), cutely headlined "Decoding . . . Fitzwater . . . ," asserted that both supporters and opponents agreed that Fitzwater could not have been talking "in purely factual terms"

about programs like Medicare, Medicaid, Social Security, or ed-
ucational aid, which were (borrowing from Wines's previous-
day story) so much a "part of the fabric of American society" that
it was difficult to imagine life without them; nor, certainly, could
Fitzwater have been thinking about small Great Society programs like Head Start, the Job Corps, or community health centers, which were widely praised by members of Bush's own
cabinet. Perhaps he was referring to AFDC, only 3 percent the
size of Social Security and Medicare; but that had been started in
the 1930s and was significantly changed by bipartisan majorities
in 1988, with Bush's blessing. This crisp assessment of social programs probably influenced subsequent critiques by others.

E. J. Dionne's story in the *Washington Post* (now moved up to
p. 1) further illustrates how interpretations can be conveyed in
news stories, especially by choice of quotations. Dionne reported that Fitzwater's statement had unleashed an angry debate; "stung" by Democratic blasts, Bush aides had backpedaled
and now insisted they were not trying to shift blame to the Democrats. Cabinet secretaries Kemp, Martin, and Louis Sullivan
(Health and Human Services) had all reformulated the attack to
concern large programs that did not work, not every aspect of
the Great Society. Fitzwater himself had seemed to back away
from his remarks, which, he said, had "played more harshly
than . . . I intended." He just meant there would not be big new
spending programs. Gephardt was quoted as accusing Bush
of perfecting the art of blame shifting; yesterday it was Willie
Horton and today it's "Jack, Bobby, Lyndon and Martin." Even
Republicans, according to Dionne, were "uneasy": Senator John
Seymour (R-Calif.) said he did not blame Johnson; it was time
for finger pointing to be set aside. Dionne noted that the attack
on the 1960s had roots in Charles Murray's book *Losing Ground,*
which argued that food stamps and Medicaid encouraged
young women to bear children out of wedlock and encouraged
fathers to avoid responsibility; Murray, in an interview, said welfare programs "masked" the long-term consequences of bad behavior, but Pat Moynihan (referring to high illegitimacy rates in
Canada, with different social programs) disagreed.

A second *Post* story (p. 9), headlined "Clinton Rips White
House's Riot Response," quoted Clinton at length. The *St. Louis
Post-Dispatch* (p. 1) reported that the administration had "re-

versed course" and quoted Gephardt's and Flynn's criticisms. The *Wall Street Journal,* too (p. 2), reported that the White House had "abruptly shifted" its stance in response to criticism.

Also on Wednesday, a broad range of newspaper editorial and op-ed pages, following the previous day's examples in the *New York Times* and *Washington Post,* came down very heavily upon Fitzwater and Bush, while the *Times* and *Post* kept at it.

Making up for Tuesday's brevity, a scornful, hard-hitting *Times* editorial, headed "The War against the Poor," alluded to Bush's "gratuitous insult" to cities in need and declared that Fitzwater's assertion "assaults the truth." The evidence, "plain to anyone willing to take an honest look," showed that the War on Poverty had helped cut poverty rates nearly in half. Instead of fighting poverty, Presidents Reagan and Bush had fought poverty programs and slashed assistance to cities dramatically. (An accompanying chart showed a steep, 60 percent drop in constant-dollar aid.) During Reagan and Bush's 1980s, poverty rates rose and then froze. The War on Poverty brought needy Americans food stamps, medical care, higher Social Security benefits, college tuition, legal services, prenatal care, and early childhood education. To denounce programs like Medicare, Head Start, and Women and Infant Children (WIC) was to deny the suffering of tens of millions who would stumble or fall without their help.

Taking a somewhat milder tack, a *Post* editorial complained that Bush and the Republicans wanted to have things both ways: they had elevated social-welfare policies of the 1960s and 1970s into a cause of the Los Angeles riots but endorsed those programs in fact even as they denounced them in history—an Orwellian maneuver. Fitzwater had called them failures, but Bush favored many (Head Start, Medicare, Medicaid, the Job Corps, compensatory education, college grants and loans). Although Fitzwater criticized "direct handouts," the *Post* said, the GOP used to advocate "cashing out" programs it considered too interventionist. The Republicans had been in power for part of the 1960s and 1970s. Some of the programs that Reagan and Bush killed or cut were products of the Nixon and Ford administrations. Some of the policies the president caricatured were clearly effective, and some were not, but as a group they were not as the White House portrayed them.

Accompanying its editorial, the op-ed page of the *Post* ran a long excerpt from Lyndon Johnson's June 1965 civil-rights speech at Howard University. In addition, a William Raspberry column called Fitzwater's comments "a low blow," "crassly political" by Fitzwater's own admission, which overlooked the contributions of a dozen Reagan and Bush years to the despair and anger that had exploded. (Of all media studied in this case, only the *Post* reported the views of a substantial number of African-American officials or commentators like Raspberry.) On pages 27–28, the *Post* featured a lengthy "Great Debate" about the Great Society, in which Fitzwater got some support from *New Republic* editor Mickey Kaus and from Walter Williams and Jack Kemp ("$2.5 trillion" [the figure kept rising] spent on social welfare had empowered bureaucrats instead of people); but Lynn Martin dodged the question, and Kemp concluded, "I don't think it was right to suggest, and I don't think he said it actually, that it caused the riot." The strongest impression was left by the negative comments of James Q. Wilson, Glenn Loury, Aaron Wildavsky, William Wilson, Joseph Califano, Robert Wood, and Olivia Golden: Fitzwater's comments were "a mistake," "ridiculous," "not edifying," "absurd"; "it doesn't make any sense."

The *Post*'s extensive Wednesday (May 6) coverage, which the *Wall Street Journal* later (May 8, p. 8) referred to as a sort of "Great Society teach-in," exemplifies the fact that the *Post* paid closer attention to the topic, over a longer period, than any other medium did, presumably because of its relatively liberal outlook and its location at the seat of the federal government and in a large African-American community.

The *Times* and *Post* were undoubtedly painful for administration officials to read. Probably even more discomforting, however, were newspapers like the *Chicago Tribune*, a generally Republican organ that had endorsed Bush in 1988 and would do so again later in 1992.[7] On Wednesday, a *Tribune* editorial declared that politicians were whittling our monumental urban problems down to their own "Lilliputian size." The Bush White House had sent Fitzwater out to blame failed policies of Democrat Lyndon Johnson's Great Society as if a quarter century since Johnson left office—all but four years of it under Republican presidents—had "counted for nothing." This slam at Bush was softened only by a balancing criticism of Democrats' condemnation of Reaganomics, a reference to the "cynicism and shallowness" of both sides, and an extensive set of policy suggestions.

Perhaps most devastating of all was the stand of the *Los Angeles Times,* a moderate Republican paper that had had an all-too-close view of the riots. In an editorial entitled "Playing Politics with a Tragedy," the *Los Angeles Times* repeated points made earlier by the *New York Times* and the *Washington Post.* It asked what programs, specifically, Fitzwater was talking about. He had said he had no list with him and had repeatedly refused to identify even one program in support of his sweeping generalization. What did he have in mind, Medicare, Medicaid, food stamps, Head Start? Granted that some programs did not work as planned, many had contributed significantly to the improvement of life for scores of millions of Americans. They had emphatically not failed, any more than Social Security or child labor laws or standards of safe food and drugs had failed. To suggest otherwise "smack[ed] . . . of implicit demagoguery." Let competing approaches be debated, but with respect for facts. The *Los Angeles Times* could not quite bring itself to stop with such flat criticism; it turned quickly to Bush's "outstanding" speech of the night before, which, "weighing words with the precision of a jeweler's scale," had condemned lawlessness while expressing compassion. But the rebuke was unmistakable.

A number of other regionally important papers spoke out against Fitzwater that same day (Wednesday, May 6). A slashing *Boston Globe* editorial criticized "childish finger pointing." The *Seattle Times* referred to "claptrap" and "demagoguery." A *St. Louis Post-Dispatch* editorial sarcastically asked, "Was it food stamps? . . . Medicaid? . . . Head Start?" and scorned "political scapegoating"; a facing-page column by Cal Thomas opposed big social programs that "club the taxpayers" but did not suggest that such programs had caused the riots. *Newsday* ran Mary McGrory's critical syndicated column. (The next week in *Newsday,* Martin Schram mocked both Bush's and Clinton's finger pointing.) The *San Francisco Chronicle* printed a column by humorist Art Hoppe, making fun of Fitzwater's charge under the heading "Welfare's a Riot." (Two days later an editorial, quoting Jack Kemp, called for action, not blame.) The *Minneapolis Star-Tribune* featured University of Minnesota staff and students defending civil-rights efforts. (Two weeks later it ran a page 1 feature in which antipoverty "pioneers" defended the legacy of the 1960s.) The day after these Wednesday editorials and columns, the *Christian Science Monitor* (May 7, p. 1) made a brief, dismissive reference to Bush's "stok[ing] the political fire." (Later it ran a column on "The Myth That Welfare Policies Don't Work.")

Still on Wednesday, May 6, evening television news shows reported continuing political battles and a Bush retreat. ABC showed mild-mannered Senate majority leader George Mitchell (D-Maine) declaring that to blame Lyndon Johnson was, "of course, absurd and ridiculous." CBS ran clips of child welfare expert Marian Edelman and former Democratic HHS secretary Joseph Califano defending Great Society programs and Representative John Lewis (D-Ga.) criticizing the "do-nothing" Bush administration; Bill Plante reported that "Mr. Bush spent the day backing away from a political firestorm." NBC cited the many newspaper editorials denouncing Fitzwater's charges and showed Jesse Jackson calling for a president with vision; John Cochran reported that Bush had been "bashing Democrats, including a dead one," and "wound up looking dumb."[8] PBS's *MacNeil-Lehrer* reported Bush as saying that Fitzwater had been grossly misinterpreted and showed Bush declaring that he would not try to assign blame; "This is no time to play the blame game." Senator Mitchell retorted that that was precisely what the administration was doing, and House Speaker Tom Foley (D-Wash.) spoke of the "very positive contribution" of 1960s programs to fairness and justice. On CNN's *Crier and Company*, Melanie Lomax commented that Fitzwater's charge was "patently absurd. . . .ludicrous."

The media reactions quoted above are typical. Scrutiny of all readily accessible national media reveals very little support for the "1960s programs did it" position during the week after Fitzwater's May 4 comment. A search of the editorial and op-ed pages of four newspapers (*Chicago Tribune, Los Angeles Times, New York Times,* and *Washington Post*) for May 5–11, for example, found a total of forty-five editorials or columns saying something about the Los Angeles riots. Of those, sixteen stated or implied a criticism of Fitzwater's remarks, while only one (Ronald Steel's, *New York Times,* May 7, mentioning "welfare dependency" amid a long list of riot causes) tended at all to support Fitzwater.

More broadly, of all the many scores of news stories, editorials, opinion columns, and commentaries in media outlets studied for this chapter, dozens opposed and only a very few supported Fitzwater. Among the media outlets that took clear evaluative stands, 77 percent opposed Fitzwater and only 8 percent supported him. Among individuals who spoke out or were quoted, 75 percent disagreed with Fitzwater and only 14 percent agreed with him (see table 3).

A few exceptions deserve comment. The *Atlanta Constitution* hedged its bets, offsetting a signed column (May 6) by its chief editorialist, Cynthia Tucker ("loose and dangerous demagoguery"; "preposterous") with a next-day Mona Charen column, "Exposing Liberal Fallacies," which spoke of social programs as "fatally flawed" and having the disastrous consequences of creating an underclass; the riot's wake-up call, if any, was that the Great Society "backfired." As we have seen, Ted Turner's CNN had broadcast Buchanan's and others' attacks on the Great Society that foreshadowed (and probably influenced) Fitzwater's charge, and it ran some strongly conservative support afterward, only partly balanced by liberal rebuttals.

The very conservative *Washington Times* (connected to Sun Yung Moon and the Unification Church) stood nearly alone, however, in its all-out defense of Fitzwater. A Friday, May 8 editorial mocked the press and professional pundits, quoted Fitzwater approvingly, and dismissed rejoinders based on pie charts, graphs, and statistics, on the grounds that they can seem to prove anything. "Fitzwater has a point," the *Washington Times* said, which Bush had made somewhat more clearly at the University of Michigan. What happened in Los Angeles was "in large part the result" of government bureaucracy displacing families, schools, and churches, whose emotional bonds it could not replace. On Sunday it followed up with an effort to counter the *Post*'s teach-in, including a fairly sober historical article by David Braaten (p. 6) but also a tendentious, page 1 "news" story, subheaded "'Great Society' Not So Great, Critics Say." This story maintained that "critics and supporters alike" now say the Great Society failed to reduce poverty and "may have made things worse," citing "$3.38 trillion" (!) of welfare spending, the enrichment of consultants, and examples of waste; "very little money actually got down to the poor." It offered extensive critical

Table 3
Reactions to Fitzwater's Charge

Negative Reactions

77% of media outlets ($n = 20$): ABC news, *MacNeil Lehrer*, *New York Times*, *Washington Post*, *Chicago Tribune*, *Los Angeles Times*, *Boston Globe*, *Seattle Times*, *St. Louis Post-Dispatch*, *Newsday*, *San Francisco Chronicle*, *Minneapolis Star-Tribune*, *Christian Science Monitor*, CBS news, NBC news, *Time*, *Newsweek*, *U.S. News*, *Business Week*, *Nation*.

75% of individuals ($n = 53$): Jerry Brown, Michael Kinsley, Michael Wines, Ann Devroy, Timothy McNulty, Bill Clinton, Willie Brown, James Desler, Ray Flynn, A. M. Rosenthal, Mary McGrory, Richard Cohen, Tony Coelho, Catherine Crier, Robert Pear, David E. Rosenbaum, E. J. Dionne, Richard Gephardt, John Seymour, Pat Moynihan, William Raspberry, James Q. Wilson, Glenn Loury, Aaron Wildavsky, William Wilson, Joseph Califano, Robert Wood, Olivia Golden, Martin Shram, Art Hoppe, George Mitchell, Marian Edelman, John Lewis, Bill Plante, Jesse Jackson, John Cochran, Tom Foley, Melanie Lomax, Cynthia Tucker, Lee Bawden, Horace Busby, Ronald Walters, R. W. Apple, Charles Schumer, Robert Beckel, Anthony Lewis, Edward Luttwak, Jim Hoagland, Charles Krauthammer, Lou Cannon, Nicholas Lemann, Peter Edelman, Robert J. Samuelson.

Mixed or Ambivalent Reactions

15% of media ($n = 4$): CNN, *Atlanta Constitution*, *Wall Street Journal*, *New Republic*.

11% of individuals ($n = 8$): Jack Kemp, Lynn Martin, William Bennett, Louis Sullivan, Cal Thomas, Ronald Steele, David Braaten, Mickey Kaus.

Positive Reactions

8% of media ($n = 2$): *Washington Times*, *National Review*.

14% of individuals ($n = 10$): Walter Williams, Dan Quayle, Mike Murphy, Edward Crane, Charles Murray, Mona Charen, Paul Gigot, William Bennett, John Sununu, Dick Armey.

Note: the stands of media outlets and individuals are listed roughly in chronological order. Individual listings include news sources, media commentators, and reporters whose reports were clearly evaluative. Since William Bennett took two conflicting positions he is listed under two categories.

quotes from Jack Kemp, Ed Crane, Abraham Ribicoff (a former Democratic senator), Thomas Sowell (Hoover Institution), and Stuart Butler (Heritage Foundation), leavened only by contrary comments from Lee Bawden of the Urban Institute and Horace Busby, former LBJ aide (Fitzwater is "a paid hack who doesn't know what he's talking about"). By the end of the story, selected quotes from Bawden, Busby, Representative Cordiss Collins (D-Ill.), and economist Sar Levitan made even them sound like critics of the Great Society. For an appearance of balance, a "Great Debate" box pitted Fitzwater and Buchanan against Clinton and Gephardt.

The *Wall Street Journal,* a major, nationally distributed organ of the U.S. financial and business communities, had probably helped inspire Fitzwater's remarks and later gave them significant, but not unequivocal, support. Besides the May 1 *Journal* editorial that opposed a flood of federal "guilt money" into ideas that had "failed," a high-octane editorial on the morning Fitzwater spoke out (May 4) had scornfully recited a long and rather odd "rosary" of alleged liberal responses to Los Angeles, including progressive taxation, condoms and asbestos removal in the schools, and ("of course") higher salaries for unionized teachers. It offered the "heretical" thought that "we have been fundamentally on the wrong track," that many of these programs do not solve problems but aggravate them. In the same issue, a George Melloan column argued that European critics had got it wrong; the War on Poverty hadn't been curtailed, it had "simply failed."

Having contributed fuel for Fitzwater's attack, the *Journal* did not altogether abandon it. On May 8, a sarcastic Paul Gigot column against "genuflect(ing)" to the Great Society compared poor Fitzwater to a vestal virgin wandering into the Roman baths; apparently he had struck a nerve at the core of the modern welfare state. A chart based on figures from the Hoover Institution's John Cogan indicated that Reagan and Bush had not cut overall spending on the poor; some programs were cut, but Medicaid "grew like Topsy," and overall spending jumped at the end of the decade. The Great Society revolutionized *how* the poor were helped, through in-kind benefits or services rather than cash. This "social engineering" by LBJ and Nixon created nonpoor lobbies for the programs and supplanted individual responsibility. On the same page of the *Journal,* William Bennett went further. Despite spending "more than $2.5 trillion" on the Great Society, life in many inner cities was worse. There were some successes, but the Great Society program taken as a whole promoted a "culture of dependency" and rewarded bad behavior. When the American people watched stores looted and people dragged from their vehicles and beaten to death, they were "seeing in part the results of a 25-year social experiment." (A box repeated and highlighted this sentence, making it starker by omitting the words "in part.")

Yet even the *Wall Street Journal* did not stand 100 percent behind Fitzwater. Of the above-mentioned pieces, only Bennett's actually suggested that Great Society programs caused the riots. And additional articles pointed the other way. A May 1, page 1 news story had offered an upbeat, pragmatic review of proposed "urban solutions" that tended to blend liberal and conservative elements (Kemp's investment cooperatives; William Wilson's car pools; the Earned Income Tax Credit; Adam Walinsky's and Kathleen Townsend's plans for students' public service; welfare and public-housing reforms). It quoted political economist Sheldon Danziger as saying that the Great Society had had successes, perhaps more than popularly believed today. (Unlike most papers, the *Journal* frequently presents a striking contrast between its news stories, which are usually moderate, sober, and carefully researched, and its very conservative editorials, which are sometimes casual about facts and shrill in tone. A recent example involves Supreme Court Justice Clarence Thomas, fiercely defended in *Journal* editorials and columns, and his accuser Anita Hill, whose charges of sexual harassment were corroborated by *Journal* news reporters.)[9] Political scientist James Q. Wilson's May 6 opinion column on black crime mentioned that the Great Society had "produced some good things" and that more funds for Head Start and the Job Corps were probably desirable. Ronald Walters's May 7 guest column even argued that "The Reagan Revolution Sparked L.A.'s Rebellion" and called it a "disservice" to blame 1960s social programs, though the column's "Counterpoint" label prevented any confusion with the *Journal*'s own position.

In any case—as table 3 indicated—most editorials, opinion columns, commentaries, and news stories in most of the major national media, especially those with the largest audiences, conveyed an impression distinctly unfriendly to Fitzwater. This was not confined to liberal or Democratic outlets, but included moderate and even some conservative Republican media as well, although the varying ideological tendencies of different media did affect the precise ways in which they handled the issue.

By Thursday, May 7 (that is, within three days of Fitzwater's remarks), most of the media action was over, and some commentators had declared an administration defeat. In the Thursday *New York Times* (p. 22), R. W. Apple Jr. tellingly reported that "senior Republican strategists," including officials of the president's campaign committee, had "laughed" at Fitzwater, and that a Republican senator had quipped, "[N]ext Marlin will blame the savings-and-loan crisis on Woodrow Wilson." In the same day's *Washington Post* (p. 30), Howard Kurtz judged that Fitzwater's criticism of Great Society programs had "clearly boomeranged." Later several weekly newsmagazines, whose publication schedules force them to specialize in summing up and interpreting news rather than reporting it, agreed. The May 18 issue of *Time* said that Fitzwater's statement was "so widely derided" that Bush quickly amended it (p. 18) or "backed away" from it (p. 36); the May 25 issue declared that Fitzwater was "pilloried so mercilessly" that President Bush had to backpedal away from his own spokesman (p. 44). In *Newsweek,* Jonathan Alter noted that blaming Lyndon Johnson "did not go over well" (May 18, p. 39).

There unfortunately exist no before-and-after data to measure precisely what effects all this rhetoric had on public opinion, but we can be sure that the American public was not convinced by Fitzwater's suggestion. On Monday, May 11, CNN reported the results of a CNN-Gallup poll conducted over the weekend. Fifty-one percent of those questioned disapproved of Bush's handling of events in the wake of the Los Angeles riots. Fifty-three percent blamed the Reagan administration's economic policies of the 1980s for racial unrest, while fewer than one-fourth agreed with the Bush administration that much of the blame rested with the Great Society programs of the 1960s. Separate surveys for CBS–*New York Times* (*NYT,* May 11, p. 1), the *Washington Post* (May 14, p. 1), and NBC–*Wall Street Journal* (*WSJ,* May 22, p. 1) all produced similar results.[10]

HAMMERING THE POINT HOME

Within three or four days after Fitzwater's May 4 press conference, the Great Society controversy had mostly disappeared from the television networks' news broadcasts. The drama of partisan confrontation seemed to be over; President Bush's May 7–8 visit to Los Angeles, a Canadian mining accident, and a space shuttle maneuver nudged the "1960s programs" story aside. During the week beginning May 11 the networks barely touched it, except for follow-ups (ABC, May 12; NBC, May 13) on how federal antipoverty programs like Head Start and community health centers actually worked—pretty well, was the main drift—in inner-city Los Angeles and elsewhere. CNN ran a "Quayle at Odds with Kemp" story May 10; on May 11 it featured a *Crossfire* brawl among Sununu, Kinsley, and Reps. Dick Armey (R-Tex.) and Charles Schumer (D-N.Y.), in which Armey charged that the Congressional Budget Office was turning out "bogus statistics." But for cable viewers, too, the Great Society story soon vanished.

Most newspapers sympathetic with President Bush and the Republicans were also quick to drop the subject. The *Los Angeles Times,* in the rest of the month after its May 6 editorial, barely mentioned the matter, except to congratulate Bush (May 9) for putting "hard-core politics" on hold after his eye-opening tour of Los Angeles, and to run a column (May 10) in which Democratic campaigner Robert Beckel said blaming the Great Society "bordered on insanity." Likewise, the *Chicago Tribune* offered only a brief editorial comment (May 12) contrasting Bush's current expressions of compassion toward victims of disorder or poverty with Fitzwater's earlier assertion. The *Wall Street Journal* editorial page fought only a minor rearguard action, speaking in a May 14 editorial of Democrats' "defensiveness" over the Great Society—they had become advocates of developers, contractors, and teachers' unions rather than the poor—and taking a swipe at the value of Great Society programs in a May 15 editorial against rap artist Sister Souljah.

The *New York Times* and *Washington Post,* however, continued a drumbeat of criticism. The *Times,* for example, cited "distinct successes" of the Great Society in a May 10, page 1 news story; it opined, in the same day's "News of the Week in Review" section, that Bush had "lapsed" in blaming the policies of long-gone Democratic administrations, and an Anthony Lewis column charged that the "unaware" and "remote" President Bush was "curiously unconnected" to Americans' desolation and desperation. A May 11 editorial referred to the "offensive" effort to "distort history." A May 15 column by Edward Luttwak ironically suggested that Bush's logic was impeccable: public assistance had kept rioters alive. Even Lawrence Mead's "new paternalism" column on May 19 (emphasizing work requirements for welfare and "shock incarceration" for young offenders) gave a friendly nod to some social programs. And a May 23 editorial took a final poke at the earlier "babbling" that had blamed the riots on Great Society programs, addiction to welfare, or even by "a fevered writer in the *National Review*" (actually the *Wall Street Journal*?) Los Angeles schools' handing out of condoms.

The *Washington Post* even more persistently hammered away at Fitzwater's remarks, offering at least one editorial or op-ed comment on the subject nearly every day for two weeks. Avoiding any appearance of excessive partisanship, most were cast as evenhanded condemnations of blame laying. After the May 5 editorial and McGrory and Cohen columns and the May 6 editorial plus Raspberry column, LBJ speech, and "Great Debate" piece, a Jim Hoagland column on May 7 criticized unworthy "finger-pointing" about "who lost Los Angeles"; American society as a whole was responsible for neglecting its cities and its disadvantaged. Charles Krauthammer (May 8) dismissed "scapegoating" of the Great Society, Reagan-Bush neglect, or the Los Angeles Police Department, suggesting instead that blame lay with the "young, brutal criminals" who terrorized the city. On the same day, Richard Cohen criticized Bush's "childish assignment of blame" to the Great Society. A May 10 *Post* editorial declared that whether some Great Society and other past programs cost too much or failed was not the issue. A same-day column by Lou Cannon criticized the soothing use of scapegoats for the riots, whether (LA police chief) Daryl Gates, the Great Society, or Reagan-Bush neglect; this "orgy of fault-finding" spared the general public and ignored Los Angeles's diffused political system that fragmented authority and accountability. And Nicholas Lemann's historical analysis of the War on Poverty (May 10, p. C1) referred to "sweeping assertions" like Fitzwater's that were "simply wrong"; ghetto pathologies predated the Great Society, and LBJ never got to try his massive assault on ghetto problems.

The onslaught continued. A May 11 *Post* column by Peter Edelman alluded to the headline, "White House Links Riots to Welfare" (*Post* writers apparently read the *Times*) and wondered whether the president was aware of people's deep and long-worsening economic pain; jobs were scarce and welfare benefits down by 40 percent (25 percent counting food stamps) since 1970 for the typical family. On May 12, Mary McGrory wrote of Bush's "first ignoble reflex" to blame Lyndon Johnson, which she called "unacceptable" in a president; she hoped Bush would "Hold . . . that Note of Compassion" he had struck at the Mount Zion Missionary Baptist Church in Los Angeles. On May 13, Robert J. Samuelson criticized indictments of Reagan-Bush neglect and scapegoating of the Great Society, arguing that government can affect deep social changes only modestly, if at all. A May 14 *Post* editorial asserted that, while some ideas after the riots of the late 1960s did not work, a few were "immensely successful," and went on to question the effects of a regime of low taxes, big deficits, and weak public policy. The *Post*'s barrage finally ended on May 18, when William Raspberry alluded briefly to George Bush's "partisan games," criticized Bush's policy proposals, and put forth his own (centering on jobs and training).

Putting together the great prominence and frequency with which the *Times* and *Post* discussed Fitzwater's charge, their unmistakably negative reaction to it, and the way that evaluative comments and negative frames appeared in news stories as well as editorials and columns, one is left with the distinct impression that editors and columnists at the *Times* and the *Post* did not merely want to refute the "1960s programs did it" argument. Rather, they seized upon it—indeed, helped to make it a big national issue—and hammered away at it, presumably in order to convince readers of the Bush administration's cynicism and irresponsibility and to advance their own political agenda.

The Great Society flap was over before newsmagazines could do much more than offer the summaries we have already noted plus a few follow-ups. *Time* ran Thomas Sancton's fact-packed, Ted Marmor–based article on welfare (May 25) and a column (June 1) in which battle-scarred CNN veteran Michael Kinsley mocked the way Bush and Buchanan had nodded to the Great Society's "good intentions"; Kinsley questioned the intentions of Bush and others who spoke of "$3 trillion" spent in twenty-five years fighting poverty, when most of that money went for sacrosanct programs like Medicare and veterans' benefits that are not aimed at the underclass. In *Newsweek* (May 18)

Mickey Kaus commented that Fitzwater had a point about welfare's enabling the underclass to form but focused on getting the ghetto poor to work by offering a "useful government job," free day care, and tax credits. *U.S. News* (May 18) issued an even-handed condemnation of "blame-laying." *Business Week* (May 18) likewise condemned "partisan recrimination" and "backbiting." *Fortune* (June 1) interviewed thirty CEOs plus sociologist Christopher Jencks on what to do about the inner-city poor.

Journals of opinion, even slower to publish, had still less to say about Fitzwater's charge. The very conservative *National Review* (May 25), without explicitly mentioning Fitzwater, declared that three decades of liberalism had "vacuumed" good qualities out of ghetto residents, transforming them into a "shiftless and criminal underclass." The neoconservative *New Republic* (May 25) said it did not, like Fitzwater, believe that welfare had "created" the underclass crisis, but it agreed with its editor Mickey Kaus that welfare was the "critical sustaining element" in the life of the underclass. The very liberal *Nation* (June 1) just printed the Bloods' and Crips' (LA gangs) $3.7 billion plan to rebuild Los Angeles.

CONCLUSION

One notable feature of this case is that a White House communication was rejected, quickly, thoroughly, and conclusively. To be sure, the communications power of the presidency was evident in the way that Fitzwater attracted media attention to an idea that had been ignored when voiced by right-wing pundits on CNN. The heavy reliance of the media upon public officials as news sources[11] is especially accentuated in the case of presidents and their spokespersons.[12] But attention does not ensure persuasive success. In this case news stories, television commentary, editorials, opinion columns, and the general public overwhelmingly rejected Fitzwater's charge. (A brief chronology is given in table 4.)

Why this rejection? One factor was undoubtedly the unpopularity of President Bush. Four surveys before the riots, in March and April 1992, found that only about 40 percent of Americans approved Bush's handling of his job.[13] Research has indicated that the persuasive power of presidents depends

Table 4
Chronology of the " '60s Programs" Dispute, 1992

Date	Event
Wed., Apr. 29	The acquittal on state charages of five policemen who beat Rodney King sparks three days of rioting in south central Los Angeles.
Thurs., Apr. 30	Clinton blames lowered federal spending. Fitzwater says such talk is outrageous.
Sat., May 2	Buchanan: utter failure of the welfare state.
Sun., May 3	Barr: the grim harvest of the Great Society.
Mon., May 4	*WSJ* editorial and column. Fitzwater makes his charge. The evening news reports it; PBS and CNN carry live discussions.
Tues., May 5	*NYT* and *WP* criticize Fitzwater in news stories and editorials; other papers quote negative reactions. Clinton, "appalled," cites "twelve years of denial and neglect." Fitzwater says he was misunderstood; cabinet secretaries pull back.
Wed., May 6	Prominent *Times* and *Post* news stories, editorials, and features attack Fitzwater's comments. Many other papers, conservative as well as liberal, editorialize against Fitzwater. Bush eschews the "blame game." TV news and discussion shows report an administration retreat.
Thurs., May 7	The *Times* and *Post* allude to a defeat for the administration. TV and newspaper coverage drops.
Sun., May 10	Newspaper wrap-up stories and columns criticize Bush and Fitzwater.
Mon., May 11	Gallup-CNN and CBS-*NYT* polls report many more Americans blame Reagan-Bush neglect than blame Great Society programs for the riots.
May 11–18	The *Post* and *Times* continue making critical references to Fitzwater's charge, while most other media are silent except for a few defenses *(WSJ)*, followups on social-welfare policies, and newsmagazine summaries.

partly upon their popular standing. Unpopular presidencies are less likely to persuade.[14]

But there is more to it than that. Research also indicates that administration officials' domination of the news media, and favorable public reactions to presidents (e.g., the "rally 'round the flag" in foreign-policy crises), both depend heavily upon the presence of a supportive elite consensus—or at least the absence of strong opposition from officials or other elites.[15] In this case there was no such supportive consensus. On the contrary, strong elite opposition arose from practically every quarter. Not surprisingly, many Democrats were upset by such a sharply partisan election-year attack on popular Democratic programs, but many Republicans, too, objected. Even the president's own cabinet members failed to back the White House charge, and once the extent of opposition became clear, the president himself and his spokesman, Fitzwater, backed away from it.[16]

This extensive elite opposition resulted both from characteristics of the particular White House communication (it was logically and factually implausible) and from a broader context related to Bush's unpopularity. While Ronald Reagan might have got away with a charge like Fitzwater's in, say, 1980 or 1984, when harsh antigovernment rhetoric was playing well, the political climate was markedly different in 1992. Unease about certain legacies of the Reagan era (huge budget deficits, the savings-and-loan disaster, increased income inequality), and especially distress over the 1990–92 economic recession, helped puncture Bush's Iraq-inflated popularity, which, by April 1992, had already fallen from its stratospheric high point of 89 percent approval to a weak 40 percent.[17] The same factors also helped create a more friendly climate for domestic government action. The Los Angeles riots, signaling something terribly wrong with America's cities, tended to reinforce these shifts. (Some businessmen, for example, began to question whether Bush could deliver either profits or social order.)

In this context, the "1960s programs did it" charge sounded to many people like a feeble excuse for domestic-policy failure, and its rejection foreshadowed the continued decline of Bush's popularity—to a miserable low point of 29 percent approval—and his decisive electoral defeat by Clinton and Perot a few months later. Thus the riots and their aftermath can be seen as defining moments of the Bush presidency.

But any enthusiasm that liberals may feel about this instance of deliberation should be tempered by recognition that its results were mainly to defend established (largely middle-class) social programs and to discredit the Bush administration, not to arrive at positive urban solutions. The broader postriot policy discourse, pinched by a scare campaign about government deficits, offered the poor little but police reinforcements, federal prosecution of King's assailants, and symbolic talk of ghetto "enterprise zones." Moreover, the media power that some may think was exercised for the good in this case could in other cases be exercised for ill.

In terms of the main themes of this book, the Riots case illustrates several features that appear to be generally characteristic of mediated deliberation in the contemporary United States.

1. The great speed of communications. In the electronic age, ideas move fast, and there is a lot of rapid interaction or *intertextuality*. Fitzwater's charge itself, made on Monday, May 4, appears to have been inspired by weekend talk shows and by the Monday morning *Wall Street Journal* editorial. Just hours after the press conference, Fitzwater's remarks were reported on television news and debated on CNN and PBS. The next morning, major newspapers joined in. Repeatedly, contending commentators answered each other immediately (on live television), or within hours. The entire affair was mostly over within three days after the press conference.[18] (In the next chapter we will see another example of speedy deliberation.)

Technological factors and publication schedules bring about a natural sequence in which different actors and different types of media outlets tend to join public deliberation in a particular order. As in this case, officials' actions or statements, reported on television and then in elite newspapers like the *Times* and the *Post,* often initiate political debate. They are followed quickly by reactions from other officials, television pundits, and newspaper editorials and opinion columns. In this instance, the whole debate was over before newsmagazines could do much more than offer brief summaries and think pieces. Journals of opinion, yet slower to publish, had even less to say. Scholarly articles and books (often important in slower, more reflective cases of deliberation) played no part here, except that previously published or forthcoming work helped to credential some experts.

2. The central role of officials and other professional communicators. In this case, like most others, deliberation in the media largely involved debate among professional communicators: public officials, experts (denizens of think tanks or nonprofit organizations, academics), and journalists (reporters, editorial and opinion column writers, talk show pundits), rather than ordinary citizens. Of the seventy individuals listed in table 4 as taking evaluative stands on Fitzwater's charge, 43 percent were professional media figures, 32 percent were officials or former officials, and 25 percent were experts. All of them occupied prominent positions enjoying special access to the media. Ordinary citizens played no visible part at all in this mediated debate; they presumably listened, thought, and talked quietly among themselves but were heard in public only later, as "numbered voices" counted by surveys after the media talk was over.[19]

3. Distinctive editorial positions. Although there was little outright support for Fitzwater's charge, reactions to it in unsigned editorials, opinion columns, and commentary (all of which tended to cluster together within each individual medium) varied significantly among different media in ways related to distinctive, long-term editorial positions. Those positions probably tended to reflect the partisan or ideological commitments and/or the economic interests of media owners and managers, as well as the nature of their audiences.[20] Although conventions of the editorial and op-ed genres now dictate efforts at apparent evenhandedness, nonpartisanship, and balance, one should not mistake the fact that the United States still has a substantially partisan press (though a quite different press, of course, from the blatantly partisan newspapers of the nineteenth century).[21]

The editorial and op-ed pages of the relatively liberal and pro-Democratic *New York Times* and *Washington Post,* for example, strongly attacked Fitzwater and defended the Great Society. On the other hand, the conservative and pro-Republican *Washington Times* and the editorial pages of the *Wall Street Journal* defended Fitzwater and attacked liberal social programs. Moderate Republican papers like the *Chicago Tribune* and the *Los Angeles Times* disagreed with Fitzwater but did so very briefly and counterbalanced their criticism with praise for President Bush. Still other newspapers (and the rather conservative CNN television network) sorted themselves out according to their general ideological stands.

4. The tendency of editorial stands to spill over into news stories. In this case, although some papers tried to stick to bland, "objective" reporting, others treated news stories in ways that conveyed a clear evaluative thrust, usually a thrust consistent with their editorial point of view. This was especially evident in the *Washington Times,* the *New York Times,* and the *Washington Post,* but it was also true of the *Chicago Tribune* and several other papers.[22] Only the *Wall Street Journal* displayed a sharp discrepancy between its editorial pages (generally pro-Fitzwater) and news pages (substantially anti-Fitzwater.)

A variety of techniques were used to slant news stories. The Fitzwater story was given page 1 prominence and big headlines, or it was buried. It was explored at length and frequently followed up, or it was quickly dropped. Stories were framed with headlines and opening paragraphs that featured either "failures" of the Great Society, or the "political" nature of Fitzwater's charge. Evaluative adjectives and adverbs, and sometimes open, unattributed evaluations, were slipped in. Most important, sources and quotations were chosen that tended to agree with the editorial line. There was a remarkable contrast, for example, between the *Washington Post*'s and the *Washington Times*' "experts" on the Great Society.

5. *The active role of certain elite media in defining issues, influencing others' stands, and shaping debate.* In this case, conservative talk shows and *Wall Street Journal* editorials probably helped provoke the whole flap by inspiring the administration to make its charge. The *Washington Post* and the *New York Times* helped create a national debate about the matter; they seized upon Fitzwater's remarks, played them up as a big story, provided critical facts and arguments to other media, and hammered away with their criticism long after other media outlets stopped.

I happen to agree with what the *Post* and the *Times* said in this particular case: Fitzwater's suggestion was stupid. But I do not believe that the *Post* and the *Times* are always right. The power that they, the *Wall Street Journal,* and other elite media appear to have, in sometimes shaping the course of political deliberation,[23] is worrisome. This is particularly a matter of concern when all or nearly all the mainstream media agree with each other, and when (as was not true of the Riots case) they are substantially out of touch with the public. The next chapter explores what happens then.

NOTES

1. The ideologically loaded term *riots* is used here, with some misgivings, in preference to *rebellion* or *uprising*, which correctly highlight political motivations but fail to capture the anomic spirit of some loot-

ing or the randomness of some violence, and in preference to *violence* or *disorder,* which sound more scientific but are too vague. (See Gooding-Williams 1993.)

2. The search included ABC network news, PBS's *MacNeil-Lehrer News Hour,* CNN news and discussion programs (information about other television network news shows was derived from the Vanderbilt Television News Archive abstracts and newspaper accounts), the *New York Times, Washington Post, Wall Street Journal, USA Today, Christian Science Monitor, Los Angles Times, Chicago Tribune, St. Louis Post-Dispatch, Miami Herald, Atlanta Constitution, Washington Times, Newsday, Boston Globe, Minneapolis Star Tribune, Seattle Times,* and *San Francisco Chronicle.* Several major newspapers *(New York Times, Washington Post, Los Angeles Times, Wall Street Journal, Chicago Tribune)* were read for a full month after the riots. The weekly issues of the main newsmagazines—*Time, Newsweek, U.S. News, Business Week*—were examined for a month or more, as were journals of commentary and opinion like *Fortune, Forbes,* the *Nation, National Review,* the *New Republic,* the Heritage Foundation's *Policy Review,* the *National Journal,* the *Atlantic,* and the *National Journal.*

3. Fitzwater, in his memoirs (1995, 344–46), admits he "stepped in it," but notes that after the 1994 elections Phil Gramm and Newt Gingrich said the same things with impunity.

4. On the concept of media framing, see Tuchman (1978), Gitlin (1980), Pan and Kosicki (1993), and Entman (1993). A striking example of two similar events (the shooting down of third-country civilian airliners by the Soviet military and the U.S. military) being framed in quite different ways in the U.S. media is given in Entman (1991). See also Entman and Rojecki (1993). Iyengar (1991) shows that media frames can affect audience reactions.

5. Parallelism between news stories and editorial stands has been surprisingly little studied. An interesting exception is a book by Arthur Rowse, a copy editor for the *Boston Traveller,* who examined thirty-one different newspapers' handling of the 1952 Nixon and Stevenson "slush fund" stories. He found that all (with the possible exception of the *New York Times*) slanted their news stories in a pro-Republican or pro-Democratic direction, and that in nearly every case the direction of bias coincided with the paper's editorial endorsement of the Republican or Democratic candidates (Rowse 1957, 127–28).

The present chapter offers additional evidence of correspondence between news slants and editorial stands in a number of media.

6. The notion that owners and publishers may influence the news contents of their publications seems to strike a very sensitive nerve among journalists and communication scholars. A reviewer of the manuscript for this book, for example, commented that the idea that

the politics of media owners explain news content is "not a view most specialists on the news media take very seriously." With the notable exceptions of Bagdikian (1992), Parenti (1993), and a few others, I am afraid the reviewer may be right.

How can this be, when most sophisticated media consumers take the influence of owners for granted? Some journalists, of course, may dismiss the idea for reasons of self-respect. They want to feel independent and autonomous. Indeed, the excellent participant-observer studies of the 1970s (e.g., Gans 1980) confirm that journalists often do feel rather autonomous. Most editors believe they have substantial leeway to follow their professional judgments; most reporters, too, feel free to pursue stories wherever they may go (subject, of course, to the negotiation of assignments and story content with editors). But it is important to see that owner and publisher influence is not at all inconsistent with journalists' subjective feelings of autonomy, because the values and beliefs of journalists (and of the editors who hire and supervise them) may already be largely in harmony with the values and beliefs of the owners— precisely because owners have the ultimate power to hire and fire.

By the same token, some scholars' rejection of the idea of owner influence on the grounds that it sounds vaguely conspiratorial or Marxist neglects the many different mechanisms (including the entirely understandable and nonconspiratorial hiring of like-minded subordinates) by which it can occur.

Perhaps the most important reason for skepticism among scholars is simply paucity of evidence. The most accessible evidence (e.g., on correspondences between news slants and editorial stands, which points toward a common factor influencing both) is rarely gathered, and more direct evidence of owner influence is extremely hard to get at. To be sure, Bagdikian (1992, esp. chaps. 2, 3, 9) and others have offered numerous compelling accounts of incidents in which owners and advertisers actively intervened to affect their publications' contents, but these can always be dismissed as atypical or "anecdotal" (despite a leading political scientist's aphorism that "the plural of anecdote is data"). Presumably many other such interventions, if they have occurred, have been carefully kept secret; the best hope of uncovering some of them is through archival research, as in recent work by Erik Devereux (1993a) and Daniel Chomsky (1995a). (D. Chomsky 1995b uses some remarkable archival evidence on cold-war and other issues, stretching over many years, to outline mechanisms of owners' and managers' control of news and editorials at the *New York Times*). But a particularly difficult problem is that certain important causal mechanisms by which owners may exert influence—for example, the intimidating "demonstration effect" of a few dramatic interventions, or the even more subtle impact of hiring like-minded staffers—are extremely difficult to study. The topic of possible owner influence deserves a major research effort.

This book analyzes only what showed up in the media, not what happened behind the scenes in newsrooms or in confidential chats between editors and publishers. Some of the patterns reported here constitute circumstantial—but of course not conclusive—evidence of owners' influence upon both editorials and news stories.

7. Newspaper endorsements for 1988 and 1992 are reported in *Editor & Publisher*, October 29, 1988, 9–11; November 5, 1988, 9–10; October 24, 1992, 9–10, 44; and November 7, 1992.

8. Kurtz (1992, A30).

9. For two *Wall Street Journal* reporters' research supporting Anita Hill against Clarence Thomas, see Mayer and Abrahamson (1994).

10. *The Wall Street Journal* poll found that, by an overwhelming 54 to 29 percent margin, people blamed urban decline on Reagan-Bush cutbacks rather than the Great Society. The *Washington Post* reported that in its poll, 55 percent said a major cause of current urban problems was the failure of Bush and Reagan to deal with inner cities. (42 percent said the "failure" of 1960s social programs was a big cause of urban distress, but some of these respondents apparently had in mind failure to fund the programs adequately; more blacks than whites gave the "failure" response.)

11. On media reliance upon officials as news sources, see, among others, Sigal (1973) and Gans (1980).

12. Presidents do not always win media attention, of course; President Clinton complained bitterly about being ignored by the media, particularly in the early days of Republican congressional ascendancy after the 1994 elections. But this merely reinforces the larger point, that when presidents are unpopular they tend to be less successful at public communication. They get less attention as well as less respect.

13. On President Bush's low popularity just before the riots, see Mueller (1994, 181–82).

14. The effect of presidential popularity upon presidents' persuasive impact is indicated in Page and Shapiro (1984; 1992, 348–50); but see Jordan (1993).

15. The role of elite consensus in affecting media coverage and presidential popularity is discussed in Hallin (1986), Bennett (1990), Nacos (1990), and Brody (1991).

16. Lance Bennett suggests that Bush and Fitzwater may have initially taken their cues from the conservative pundit corps without understanding that outrageous or silly remarks, though standard fare for commentators, become "news"—and therefore fair game for overwhelming attacks by opponents—when enunciated by public officials.

An indexing norm therefore kicked in, journalistic cues informed the public that Bush was out of line, the administration backed off, and (except for the *Times'* and *Post's* continuing to pile on) the story was over (personal communication, October 21, 1993).

17. On the steep slide in President Bush's popularity after the Iraq war—which was also related to Saddam Hussein's continued hold on power, the widely televised plight of Kurdish refugees, and revelations of earlier U.S. aid to Hussein and failure to warn him firmly against invading Kuwait—see Mueller (1994, 89–92, 179–82, 378).

18. Approximately 90 percent of all the television and newspaper references to Fitzwater's charge—including wrap-up and recap stories—appeared within seven days after his press conference.

19. On limitations of "numbered voices" in polls, see Herbst (1993). The absence of a visible public role in mediated discourse, however, does not at all mean that ordinary citizens are left out of the deliberative process. While we have only limited evidence about the citizenry in this case, the poll results indicate that most citizens came to a judgment (a predominantly negative one) on Fitzwater's charge, a judgment that was, in a sense, the chief result of this instance of deliberation. Many citizens undoubtedly learned about the charge and the responses to it through the media, assessed the facts and ideas offered by professional communicators (especially those they trusted), discussed the matter among themselves, and came to a conclusion. This is precisely the way that chapter 1 suggested mediated deliberation could work successfully by and for the general public.

20. The clustering of each publication's unsigned editorials, opinion columns, and other commentary around a more or less unitary editorial position I take to be an empirical fact, reasonably well established by the evidence in this and the previous chapter and by informal observation over the years. The durability over time of particular media's distinctive editorial positions, too, I consider to be an empirical fact, inferred from longtime media watching by myself and others. (My forty-odd years of reading the *New York Times* and *Wall Street Journal,* for example, has produced an indelible impression of great editorial continuity, despite numerous changes of editors and columnists.)

It is harder to be confident about the reasons why different media take the positions they do. The durability of publications' stands suggests that fairly fundamental factors, involving owners, advertisers, and/or audiences, are probably at work, but it is not easy to sort them out—or even to distinguish between owners' adherence to industrial-sector, profit-oriented factors as opposed to their own values and preferences. This is an important area for future research.

21. For further evidence on the continuing existence of a funda-

mentally partisan press, see Devereux (1993a). Such partisanship is now hidden behind "objectivity," however, and is quite muted—perhaps to the detriment of public deliberation—in comparison with the United States of the nineteenth century, when openly partisan newspapers with sharply differing views argued against each other, educating and mobilizing the citizenry. See Lasch (1990) and Carey (1989).

22. Again, it is important to bear in mind that a correspondence between news slant and editorial position could come about through a variety of causal mechanisms, some of which (especially the appointment by owners of like-minded editors who tend to hire and promote like-minded commentators and reporters) can be noninterventionist, unconscious, and nonviolative of journalists' feelings of autonomy or of the news/editorial "wall of separation."

23. The impact of the *Journal*, the *Times*, and the *Post* upon other media and upon the Bush administration is evidenced in this case by time asymmetries (they spoke first), by echoes of their language—sometimes verbatim—elsewhere, and by explicit references to their stands.

Another example of elite newspapers shaping debate: shortly after disposing of Fitzwater, the *Times* and the *Post* seized upon a brief reference in a speech by Dan Quayle to the *Murphy Brown* television show's treatment of single motherhood and used it to ridicule Quayle, helping to spark a summer-long fight about "family values."

FOUR

Zoe Baird, Nannies, and Talk Radio

with Jason Tannenbaum

In the Riots case, survey evidence suggests that most Americans found the mediated discourse—which was generally critical of Fitzwater's charge—to be helpful and persuasive. At least most people agreed, in the end, with its predominant conclusion. But what happens if public officials and other professional communicators in the mainstream media are, in some relevant respect, highly unrepresentative of the public for whom and to whom they speak? What if they fail to reflect the values held by most ordinary Americans? The following case suggests that such unrepresentativeness can indeed occur, but that—at least under certain limited circumstances—it can be overcome by a populist uprising through alternative communication channels.

INITIAL MEDIA SUPPORT FOR BAIRD

On December 24, 1992, President-elect Bill Clinton announced that he would nominate Zoe Baird to become the first female attorney general of the United States. After promising a diverse cabinet that would "look like America," but then announcing a number of male appointees, Clinton had come under pressure from feminist groups to appoint more women. In Baird Clinton did choose a woman, but not one with strong ties to the women's movement; Baird was a high-powered corporate lawyer who had worked for General Electric and the Aetna Insurance Company. Nonetheless, women's groups and most others reacted positively to the Baird nomination.

Most media reports were quite favorable.[1] The *New York Times*, in particular, sounded positively ecstatic. An editorial declared: 77

Personable and smart, experienced in the ways of the Justice Department and White House, Ms. Baird more than vindicates President-elect Clinton's determination to put a woman at the head of the federal legal establishment. . . . The most impressive nomination yesterday was Ms. Baird's. (Dec. 25, p. A30)

The *Times'* page 1 news story quoted Clinton to the effect that Baird was "tough, tenacious and gifted"; she would put together a team of excellent lawyers, lift morale, solve problems, and restore a sense of movement to the Justice Department. Anthony Lewis's *Times* column (p. 31) called Baird "the most inspired stroke of Bill Clinton's Cabinet-making."

The *Chicago Tribune*, basing its story on the *New York Times* news service, noted mixed reactions to the changes coming at Justice ("many career employees were thrilled and some were alarmed") but referred to Baird as "an accomplished and by all accounts brilliant lawyer" and quoted Clinton on her being tough, tenacious, gifted, and a "very, very able manager." The *Atlanta Constitution* mostly just described Baird's background, emphasizing her "powerhitter" mentors, Lloyd Cutler and Warren Christopher, but also said she was on "one of America's fastest legal tracks" and that *Business Week* had named her as one of the fifty top women in business. CNN's *Inside Politics* (Dec. 30) offered a bouquet of testimonials. *Newsweek*, twice in one edition (Jan. 4, 1993), called Baird "brilliant."

Only a bit of negative material found its way into early media reactions to Baird. The *Los Angeles Times'* December 25 story on Clinton's final cabinet appointments briefly mentioned public-interest lawyers' reservations about Baird because of Aetna's efforts to limit corporate liability for defective products and noted that Clinton had passed over Brooksley Born, whom many women's organizations had supported. On the same day, another page 1 *Los Angeles Times* story quoted Clinton's praise for Baird (a "dynamic, talented and innovative lawyer") and said she had been "acclaimed as a rising star" in legal circles and by government insiders but noted "unhappy rumblings" from public-interest groups over her corporate ties and the product liability issue; it also cited Baird's lack of experience with criminal law, government service, or administration of large organizations. A piece by Michael Isikoff in the *Washington Post* (p. A23) took a similar tack, saying Baird was hailed by associates as brilliant, personable, hardworking, and innovative, but citing "a number of potential handicaps" including lack of government experience and liberal interest groups' concerns because she had helped General Electric fend off allegations of procurement fraud and had backed Aetna's efforts to restrict jury awards in lawsuits against corporations. (The *Dallas Morning News* ran a truncated version of this *Post* story, noting Baird's lack of experience.)

A few days later (Jan. 6), policy-based opposition to Baird became more open when *USA Today* quoted Ralph Nader as saying that Baird was a disappointing choice who had "stood by corporate interests against consumer interests." It also quoted Scott Armstrong of Taxpayers against Fraud as concerned that Baird might be "unwilling to pursue corporate crime." Subsequent stories and columns in *USA Today*, the *Los Angeles Times*, and the *Washington Post* pursued these themes. Eventually—on the same day (Jan. 13) that Terry Eastland's admiring *Wall Street Journal* column was headlined "An Attorney General [that departing Republican vice president Dan] Quayle Could Love"—the *New York Times* took note of the liberal objections that had "tempered the euphoria" about Baird, and summarized the criticisms in detail, adding that Baird had lobbied Congress to insulate companies like GE from whistle-blower lawsuits. (This curiously delayed *Times* piece by David Johnston, a reporter who covered the Justice Department beat and who was about to break the illegal-immigrant story about Baird the following day, may have represented a last-minute effort to warn of trouble ahead and/or to distance the *Times* from its former favorite in the light of what was coming.)[2] Still, no one was predicting any difficulty for Baird beyond the possibility that Nader might testify against her.

As these quiet grumblings foreshadowed, although Baird's nomination was quite well received and provoked little open opposition, it later proved vulnerable because no particular constituency stood strongly behind her. Baird was not the first choice of feminists or liberals. Republicans, reassured by Baird's corporate ties and her position on tort reform, were generally pleased with the nomination (especially as contrasted with possible liberal alternatives) but were unlikely to go out on a limb to defend a Democratic president's nominee when she later ran into trouble. Thus Baird won widespread approval, but no group would back her in a fight.

THE DOMESTIC-WORKER PROBLEM

On Thursday, January 14, 1993, a front-page *New York Times* story revealed that Zoe Baird had employed two Peruvians living illegally in the United States as her baby-sitter and part-time driver for about two years. Anonymous "transition officials" were quoted as saying that the couple began working for Ms. Baird in the summer of 1990, when she was about to take her job at Aetna; the wife continued to help care for Baird's three-year-old son until shortly after the 1992 election. Transition officials also said Ms. Baird and her husband (only later in the story identified as Paul Gewirtz, a constitutional-law scholar at Yale Law School) had been told by a lawyer that it was not possible to pay Social Security taxes to people who did not have a right to work here. Baird and Gewirtz did not pay until they made a lump-sum payment "this month."

The story noted that a 1986 law made it illegal knowingly to hire an illegal alien; employers are required to verify citizenship. Individual homeowners are liable for civil penalties, including fines up to three thousand dollars for each violation. Transition officials said Baird believed she was acting legally because she was sponsoring the woman's application for citizenship, but immigration lawyers said applicants could not be legally employed until receiving a visa and work permit, which the Peruvians did not have. Transition aides and "government officials" gave contradictory accounts of whether Baird had completed various steps (Labor Department certification? Immigration and Naturalization Service approval?) toward a visa and work permit, and whether the Peruvian couple had ended their employment voluntarily or the woman had been dismissed shortly after the election, perhaps to clear the matter up as Baird prepared for a possible job with the government. Transition officials said that "recently" lawyers helping Baird prepare for confirmation hearings had told her that she should have made Social Security payments, and she wrote a check to the Treasury for the full amount.

Although the *Times* story reported most of the facts that

eventually proved very damaging to Baird, the story as a whole did not convey an impression of serious trouble. It noted that the hiring was potentially "embarrassing" (a phrase later echoed in other media) for a top law enforcement officer who would supervise the INS but said that, in practice, the immigration service rarely prosecutes people who employ illegal aliens in their homes. It emphasized that Baird had volunteered information about the couple to Mr. Clinton (before she was named), to the Federal Bureau of Investigation, to Senator Joseph Biden (D-Del.), chair of the Judiciary Committee, and to Senator Orrin Hatch (R-Utah), a senior committee member. Biden told the *Times* that he was satisfied with her explanations; he had alerted Democratic committee members Kennedy, Metzenbaum, and Feinstein, and he said that—barring an FBI report to the contrary—"this is not a deal breaker" that should keep her from being attorney general. Transition spokesman Ricki Seidman said Baird had fully disclosed and explained the situation during the selection process; "she will be an excellent Attorney General."

Clearly, then, the bare fact that Baird had hired illegal aliens had not created a storm in elite circles that would foreclose her nomination or confirmation. The *Times* article was rather bland and matter-of-fact, even antiseptic, in tone. Its heavy reliance on congressional and transition officials—who were presumably consulted after the *Times* got a leak from Justice or elsewhere—implied acceptance of their point of view. In fact, except for brief references to the slightly conflicting comments of "government officials" (members of the departing Bush administration, a careful reader would note), the story gave no indication of negative reactions and no cues that readers should be outraged. As we saw in the Riots case, the *Times'* news stories are quite capable of cuing reader outrage when they wish to do so.

COMPLACENCY AMONG OFFICIALS AND THE MEDIA

The *Times* story, though appearing on page 1, tended to frame Baird's hiring of illegal aliens as a minor matter that would not threaten the nomination. The same impression was conveyed by television news coverage that evening. ABC news, for example, ran a short segment in the middle of its program. While making clear that the violations were against the law, it gave no hint that they might be considered serious. Clinton spokesman George Stephanopoulos and Senator Biden were reported as not thinking it would be a problem, and Senator Hatch, the leading Judiciary Committee Republican, agreed: "Technically, she didn't dot every 'i' and cross every 't'—that should not be held against her when she otherwise is very qualified." An ABC reporter declared that, although against the law, it was "not unusual" for affluent people to hire low-paid illegal aliens for domestic work and showed a clip of a resident of Bel Air (a posh Los Angeles suburb) saying, "I think it's extremely common. Extremely common." The reporter closed the story:

> A top immigration official told ABC news these violations are as common as shoes and impossible to police. That may help explain why the revelations about Zoe Baird, however embarrassing to the nominee, are not expected to jeopardize her nomination.

Other networks reacted similarly. CBS news devoted only twenty seconds to the story. NBC allocated nearly two and a half minutes, but after quoting Stephanopoulos it spent most of its time on a debate about immigration reform. CNN barely mentioned the story on *Crossfire* and *Inside Politics* and did not cover it in any of its newscasts.

One reason for the mild reaction seems clear: the media were relying on government officials, of both parties, who minimized the matter. The views expressed in the media reflected, or indexed,[3] the views of official Washington. It is hard to imagine that the problem would have been treated so lightly if the disclosure had led to fierce opposition on the Judiciary Committee. Nor, as we will discuss further below, did the values of journalists themselves appear to be affronted.

On the morning of Friday, January 15, the nation's newspapers other than the *Times* had their first opportunity to deal with the illegal-alien story. Their coverage—or noncoverage—makes clear that most did not consider the story very significant. The *Boston Globe* and the *Dallas Morning News* did not mention the Baird matter at all. Other papers, such as the *Atlanta Constitution* and *USA Today,* played it as a minor matter that, according to members of the Judiciary Committee, would not undermine the nomination.

Some papers gave the story more attention but still conveyed a distinct lack of outrage. The *Los Angeles Times* ran a page 1 headline, "Hiring of Illegal Aliens by Baird Sparks Little Uproar . . . Senators Signal Justice Dept. Nominee Won't Be Harmed by Doing What Many Working Parents Do." The story asserted, without documentation, that Baird had done what "millions" of other upper-middle-class American working parents have done; "such violations of immigration and tax laws are committed with scarcely a second thought by the most law-abiding, civic-minded parents—model citizens." It cited Judiciary Committee members Biden, Hatch, and Simpson (R-Wyo.) for the proposition that Baird's prospects for confirmation appeared unharmed and went on to discuss general issues of immigration and child care. Buried in the article were comments that Baird had earned more than five hundred thousand dollars a year from Aetna; that many illegal immigrants were being exploited and were perhaps driving down wages for American workers; and that in 1986 Congress specifically rejected a "Beverly Hills" provision to exempt domestic workers from immigration laws.

The *Wall Street Journal,* too, gave the story page 1 play but generally supported Baird. "It is a dilemma faced by thousands of baby-boom parents," the story began: "Do you hire a nanny who seems loving and reliable but who is an illegal immigrant? . . . Like many others, Zoe Baird chose to hire the illegals." To thousands of working families struggling to find decent child care, the reporters suggested, Baird's crime appeared to rank with jaywalking. They did quote Ellen Miller of the Center for Responsive Politics ("This is a crime of the rich") and Ralph Nader ("violating the immigration laws and the tax laws by a lawyer . . . should be a disqualification from the office"), but such sources were not likely to carry much weight with the *Journal*'s affluent readers; the article reminded them of Nader's previous opposition to Baird as probusiness. It went on to quote extensive support for Baird and noted in passing that Baird and her husband showed a combined annual income of $660,345 for 1992 and had a net worth of $2.3 million.

The *Washington Post,* barely mentioning in its page 1 Clinton story that Stephanopoulos had been "besieged" with questions about Baird, ran two Baird stories on page 14. One said that Senate Judiciary Committee members "foresaw no roadblocks" to confirmation, quoting Senators Simpson (one of the authors of the 1986 law) and Biden. Although this article also quoted Nader's opposition, it went on to cite immigration lawyers as saying that what Baird and Gewirtz did "is standard practice in Washington, D.C." The second article, gently headlined "In Washington Area, Hiring of Illegal Help Meets Mutual Needs," traced some social repercussions, such as employers' insistence that workers be tested for tuberculosis and AIDS, the lack of health benefits or job security, and cases of economic and even sexual exploitation. But it gave no indication that the illegal-alien issue was a major problem for Baird.

The *New York Times*, following up its previous day's revelations, ran two Baird stories on page 15. According to one, headlined "Clinton Not Fazed . . . ," press secretary Dee Dee Myers said that Clinton had been aware of Baird's hiring of the illegal aliens but did not think it was a problem. The second article reported that the disclosure had raised few eyebrows in Baird's affluent Prospect Hill neighborhood in New Haven, Connecticut, where a judge, a congresswoman, and a generous supply of doctors and lawyers lived, and where "both husband and wife often work at powerful jobs."

In unusual contrast with their news coverage, however, both the *Post* and—most surprisingly—the *Times* ran editorials questioning the suitability of Baird's nomination.[4] The *Times* editorial, headlined, "Needed: Answers from Ms. Baird," stated that Baird apparently carried out "a clear, prolonged violation of the immigration law. . . . This country needs the assurance that . . . the Justice Department will be in the hands of someone with unimpeachable standards." It warned Senator Biden that his reputation could not stand another "tardy, unfocused" inquiry like the Clarence Thomas hearings and concluded that "anything short of providing an honest and convincing explanation has to disqualify Zoe Baird." The *Post* said that Baird was under a "visible cloud" for her violations of law. It advised Clinton and Baird to "think carefully about the deeply troubling condition into which the Justice Department has fallen and ask whether an attorney general with this limited but conspicuous mark on her own record is the right person to undertake the great cleansing and rehabilitation the department requires."

The *Chicago Tribune* was more sympathetic to Baird; it editorialized that the violation merited serious questioning, but, "while the laws are indeed on the books and violations are frequent, the government almost never prosecutes anyone for the sort of thing Zoe Baird did. It would seem strange indeed if such a law should become a bar to public office."

The limited editorial reactions by newspapers, then, were mixed; they, and some tidbits buried on the inside news pages, offered at least a mild foreshadowing of trouble to come. But the headlines and the main thrust of virtually all the news stories, based heavily on official sources, presented a picture of the illegal-alien issue as nothing more than a minor embarrassment. This was even more true of television, upon which most Americans rely for political news. Neither ABC, CBS, CNN, nor NBC mentioned the Baird story once in their newscasts on January 15. It seems unlikely that they would have ignored it, a day after the story broke, if they had felt that a major scandal was threatening the nomination.

Much the same pattern continued to hold for the next three days, from Saturday, January 16, through Monday, January 18. Coverage was minimal, especially on Sunday and Monday; newspapers and television generally relied on official sources and played the story as no more than a minor embarrassment. They briefly reported then-obscure Representative Newt Gingrich's (R-Ga.) call for Clinton to withdraw the Baird nomination if she broke the law but noted that Senate Judiciary Committee members doubted her confirmation would be derailed. They reported Baird's payment of a twenty-nine-hundred-dollar fine to the INS for employing the illegal aliens, noting statements supporting Baird from Clinton and from Judiciary Committee leaders Biden and Hatch; Hatch said he hoped this was the "final step" to confirmation. Baird came up in some discussions of Clinton's transition troubles, along with Haiti, Iraq, gays in the military, a middle-class tax cut, the deficit, and corporate funding of a scheduled party for Commerce secretary-designate Ron Brown. But much more attention was devoted to the upcoming inauguration and to Clinton's bus trip from Virginia to Washington, D.C.

Only the *Washington Post*'s news coverage raised serious questions. On Saturday, Michael Isikoff's page 1 story, headlined "Is Baird's Initial Luster Fading?" listed "concerns" among committee staff members, transition officials, and advocacy groups about matters other than illegal aliens: Baird's lack of experience as a prosecutor or with civil-rights law, the criminal-justice system, or government service; her development and advocacy while at Aetna of Quayle's "tort reform" proposals, which Clinton had attacked as "dramatically tilted toward big polluters, manufacturers and insurance companies"; and her work defending GE against allegations of defense contract fraud and proposing restrictions on whistle-blower suits. On page 12, the *Post* added a jab at the illegal-alien issue, emphasizing that as attorney general Baird would supervise the INS (whose employees could be disciplined for breaking the law she apparently broke) and the tax division of the Justice Department (where failure to file taxes disqualifies job applicants).

On various editorial and op-ed pages a scattering of negative references to Baird appeared, including Clarence Page's criticism of Clinton administration "yuppie crimes" and Jerry Knight's attack on the notion that a prospective attorney general didn't know the law about immigrants and taxes or that a twelve-thousand-dollar-a-week couple couldn't afford to obey the rules: "People like this give yuppies a bad name." But more visible was strong editorial support from the *Los Angeles Times* and the *Wall Street Journal.* The *Los Angeles Times* editorial asked whether this minor scandal should disqualify Baird from being attorney general: "We think not." The *Journal*, confirming a quiet elite realignment in which Republicans were becoming Baird's strongest defenders while a few Democrats had doubts, attacked its editorial foes at the *New York Times* and *Washington Post:*

> It appears that Zoe Baird will be confirmed as Attorney General. . . .This outcome is consummately to be desired, and is in particular an enormous boon to Bill Clinton. . . .
>
> Slowly word leaked that she had lived too long in the real world, even to the point of endorsing Dan Quayle's legal reforms and other politically incorrect things. . . .What basically had been going on here is an attempt by the Democratic left to roll Mr. Clinton. . . .
>
> What was found was a violation of the immigration laws on domestic help, an area of law so complicated, so unrealistic and so morally ambiguous that in the normal course of business the government doesn't care to enforce it. . . .

Of course someone can protest, "but it's the law." If this kind of offense bars an otherwise qualified nominee, speeding tickets and parking violations cannot be far behind.

Television interview and discussion shows gave Baird little attention, and what they gave was mostly favorable. On CNN's conservative *Capital Gang*, Mona Charen called the illegal-alien problem "pretty minor." Robert Novak said, "I think it is a ridiculous offense. . . . All of Al's [fellow pundit Hunt's] high-tone social friends have illegals." Senator Paul Simon (D-Ill.) flatly stated that the illegal hiring was not enough to stop Baird from being confirmed. Near the end of ABC's *This Week with David Brinkley*, Sam Donaldson declared that Baird's action was against the law, but not a terrible crime. George Will was more agitated over the idea that if this were a Republican the Democrats would be screaming than he was concerned with the actual offense. Only Cokie Roberts (reacting, as it later became clear, like many working women) attacked Baird's credibility: "I'd like to know what she was paying them, frankly, because she made enough money to hire Mary Poppins. . . . [T]he idea that the only people that you could get under these circumstances are people that you have to hire illegally is just not the case with somebody who makes that much money." But this was a brief, solitary criticism. On CNN's *Newsmaker Sunday*, Senators Robert Dole (R-Kans., the minority leader) and George Mitchell (D-Maine, the majority leader) indicated that there would be questions and perhaps a delay beyond Tuesday's scheduled hearing, but they foresaw no real difficulty with confirmation.

Quite atypical amid all this complacency was a Saturday *New York Times* opinion piece by Russell Baker, who seemed to sense the upcoming crisis and to understand its roots:

> The Baird Story is rife with trivialities of the sort that may not amount to a hill of beans to higher Washington but tend to infuriate the masses who telephone talk-radio stations. . . . Angry questions poured from the radio: Didn't know? Well how come, if she didn't know, she suddenly paid up all the previously unpaid taxes after the Attorney General job came through? (Jan. 16, 1993, p. 21)

Thus Baker, presumably writing on Friday, January 15—almost immediately after the illegal-alien disclosure—already saw that the public considered this a serious issue. As he indicated, call-ins to radio talk shows were already expressing anger. Yet, in all the media examined for this chapter through Monday, January 18, no other newspaper or television story alluded to public outrage over the nomination. Why not? Because no "scientific" evidence (i.e., polls) had yet been gathered? Because of simple inattention? Or was Baker on to something when he went on to suggest that the press was out of touch with ordinary Americans—that reporters no longer belonged to the working class but were success-oriented professionals, living in Georgetown and Chevy Chase, entertaining senators, playing golf, and sending their children to private schools?

In sum: by Monday, January 18, four days after the *New York Times* broke the illegal-immigrant story, the major media had offered only a sprinkling of serious criticisms of Baird and—relying heavily on Senate Judiciary Committee officials—had almost universally predicted that she would be confirmed as attorney general. Official Washington and most media elites (in part, perhaps, because of their economic class position, which was quite different from that of most Americans) saw little problem. Hire illegal aliens? Fail to pay Social Security taxes? No big deal, everybody does it. Yet four days later the Baird nomination was withdrawn in the face of strong opposition. What happened?

THE PUBLIC UPRISING

Something was going on beyond the Beltway that surrounds Washington: a lot of ordinary Americans were upset about Baird, and many were expressing their anger. As we have seen, the major, traditional, mainstream media, themselves rather complacent about the matter, did not report this. But in fact a popular uprising was under way, expressed through letters, phone calls, and faxes to newspaper editors and members of Congress, and especially through calls to local radio talk shows.

As WPOP-AM (Hartford, Connecticut) talk show host Judy Jarvis later put it:

From the moment I raised Zoe Baird's name on my radio talk show last week [i.e., before Monday, Jan. 18] I knew that my Washington friends were wrong. My calls from the real America

were overwhelmingly against Baird. . . .[It] was a very big deal indeed, no matter how much the Beltway said otherwise. Here was a
crime . . . that Main Street could relate to. Store owners, working
moms and dads, legal and illegal workers, I got calls from all of
them, across the political and economic spectra, demanding that
the nation's top cop not be guilty of a crime they knew better than
to commit.

　Baird's offense, callers said, was avoidable by a woman making
half a million dollars a year in a state going through a crippling
and pervasive recession. How could she not find an out-of-work
Connecticut couple to do the job? (Jarvis 1993)

Jarvis declared that the Judiciary Committee, which had embar-
rassed itself by failing to take Anita Hill's allegations about
Clarence Thomas seriously, had been out of touch then and was
out of touch now.

　As several journalists eventually reported, radio talk show
hosts all over the country had similar experiences.[5] Diane Rehm
of WAMU-FM (Washington, D.C.) said thirteen of her twenty
callers on Monday, January 18 insisted that Baird withdraw;
only three supported the nominee. "They said, 'My God, she
earns so much money, her husband's a Yale law professor, she's
been counseling all kinds of corporations.' There wasn't much
sympathy." A Boston host remarked, "I don't think the average
schmo says, 'Hey, I know 15 people who have Peruvian live-in
nannies.'" Susan Estrich (KABC, Los Angeles) said, "The phones
went crazy . . . I found a fire already raging." Jon Matthews
(KPRC-AM, Houston) reported that his show was swamped with
calls. "It's hard to identify with somebody who has that type of
income and assets breaking the law. People read a lot of arrogance into that." Marjorie Clapprood (WHDH, Boston) estimated that two-thirds of her calls were from women who had
been through the rigorous process of finding day care, and who
were having none of it. Michael Jackson (KABC, Los Angeles)
judged that at least 75 percent of his callers wanted Baird to step
aside, and most identified themselves as Democrats.

　It is important to our argument that this talk show rebellion
got started well before any substantial conflict over Baird appeared in the mainstream media. Our main point is that a relatively autonomous popular uprising—based on the bare facts of

the case as reported on television, and reinforced by hearing fellow citizens' anger on talk radio[6]—overcame the complacency of Washington officials and media elites, changed public discourse, and overturned Baird's sure-thing confirmation.

That the uprising was an independent causal factor is indicated by the sequence of events. As Russell Baker's observation and the Jarvis and Rehm examples make clear, talk show call-ins started early, before the hearings were held and before substantial opposition surfaced in the mainstream media. Moreover, the call-ins seem in this case to have been largely spontaneous, not generated by talk show hosts. Rush Limbaugh, nemesis of the Clinton administration, was relatively quiet this time. Anti-Baird calls poured in to hosts of all political persuasions, including liberals like Susan Estrich, who had been Democrat Michael Dukakis's presidential campaign manager in 1988. Several hosts later commented on the spontaneity of these call-ins; some indicated they would rather have changed the subject. And even those who happily stoked the fires, like Judy Jarvis (a self-described Clinton voter who was "outraged" about Baird), point out that they succeeded only because there was substantial resonance among the public.[7] White House aide Paul Begala, complaining about talk show "arson" on other issues, acknowledged that the Baird case was "spontaneous combustion."[8]

But of course the world is not always neat and orderly: the popular uprising also interacted with, and became entangled with, certain elite-level processes, especially the crucial Senate confirmation hearings that began on Tuesday, January 19. The hearings made the Baird affair much more salient, broadening and intensifying public opposition. Millions of Americans, through live broadcasts on C-Span and CNN, or through news-clips elsewhere, got a chance to see Baird perform at length in a relatively unmediated setting, and many did not like what they saw. But this setting was only *relatively* unmediated; senators' questions framed Baird's performance. And those questions, particularly from Chairman Biden, had a somewhat sharper edge than had been evident in earlier comments by Judiciary Committee members. It may be that warnings from the *New York Times* and others against a committee whitewash, together with indications of lawyers' and liberal groups' policy-based disillusionment with Baird as well as the outraged phone calls from the general public, all helped stiffen committee Democrats' back-bones.[9]

Most newspapers on Tuesday morning previewed Baird's hearing before the Judiciary Committee. The *Atlanta Constitution, Dallas Morning News, Washington Post, Los Angeles Times,* and *USA Today* all ran inside-page articles recapping Baird's violations of law but continuing to predict her likely confirmation. However, Mary McGrory's page 2 *Washington Post* preinauguration piece quoted three ordinary Americans against Baird (a rare use of non-elite sources), and several other articles outside the confines of standard news fare sounded alarms: the *Los Angeles Times'* strongly negative column by small businessman Walter Kitchenman; the same newspaper's story warning that rushed hearings could lead to a Bert Lance–style humiliation; the *Boston Globe's* skeptical editorial calling for a "full explanation"; *USA Today's* sarcastic Joe Urschel opinion piece; and a powerful *Washington Post* column by law professor and former Justice Department official Patricia King, who wanted no more "tainted and tawdry" attorneys general.

In the Tuesday hearings themselves, about half of the six hours focused on Baird's hiring of the Peruvian couple. Several senators, though courteous and respectful toward Baird and full of praise for her qualifications and her poised, professional demeanor, asked persistent questions. Baird admitted that she knew at the time that it was against the law to hire illegal aliens and said she deeply regretted it.

> I made a mistake . . . I was wrong. . . .Quite honestly, I was acting, at that time, really more as a mother than as someone who would be sitting here designated to be Attorney General. . . .I gave too little emphasis to what was described to me as a technical violation of the law.

Baird took full responsibility for the violations, but at the same time declared it was her husband who dealt with the immigration lawyers.

Chairman Biden commented on the human ability to rationalize, to "justify what you know is not right." He declared that millions of Americans have trouble taking care of their children, on one-fiftieth of Baird's income, and do not violate the law. Senator Thurmond (R-S.C.) insisted that Baird admit that she did wrong and say that she was sorry, that she was repentant. Senator Simpson spoke of "elitism" and "flouting of the law." True, Senator Kennedy (D-Mass.) praised Baird's background, and Senator Hatch—the kindest questioner—said he chose to accept that the hiring was an "honest mistake," but Baird did not receive the outpouring of vote pledges that nominees hope for.

Many Americans who saw the hearings on cable television reacted negatively and strongly. Around the country, call-in lines to radio talk shows lit up. Members of Congress were deluged with telephone calls. Senator Howard Metzenbaum (D-Ohio) reported 50 negative calls and none positive; Senator Paul Simon got 165 calls against Baird and only 7 for her (*Washington Post,* Jan. 20, p. 1; *Boston Globe,* Jan. 20, p. 1). Staffers later acknowledged that, through Tuesday, Senator Specter (R-Pa.) got 800 calls against Baird and fewer than 40 for her; Senator Biden got fully 1,511 against and only 53 for (*Washington Post,* Jan. 21, p. A3).

Phone calls to politicians and radio talk shows, of course, are not necessarily representative of public opinion. Talk show callers tend to be atypical in motivations and demography.[10] Indeed, callers during the beginning of the Clinton administration were generally quite *un*representative of the public as a whole: they tended to be a "vocal minority," older, more male, more apt to be retired, more conservative, and more anti-Clinton than the average American.[11]

Still, in the Baird case, the phone calls reflected a large and diverse segment of the public. This is evident not only from hosts' and reporters' descriptions of the callers as diverse (liberal, conservative, Republican, Democrat, young, and old, including an unusually high proportion of women), but also because survey data indicate that many Americans shared their concerns. A national survey of a representative sample of citizens, which Gallup, CNN, and *USA Today* conducted on Monday and Tuesday, January 18–19, found that 51 percent considered it a "major concern" when told that Baird had hired illegal aliens to work in her home in violation of the law, while 33 percent called it a minor concern and only 15 percent said it was not a concern at all.[12]

Our point is not that the phone callers constituted a random sample of the public (surely not: almost certainly they were more knowledgeable, more negative, and more intense, since those who don't know or don't care are unlikely to call in), but that they reflected the values of average Americans more accurately than did the elite consensus of the time.[13]

In Tuesday evening reports on the hearings, television news for the first time indicated that Baird's violations of law might constitute a serious scandal, though not enough to prevent confirmation. This switch coincided with an apparent change in officials' attitudes, as manifested by the relatively tough questioning Baird received in the hearings, and with signs of the popular uprising, particularly reports from senators that constituents' telephone calls were running heavily against the nominee. (Presumably it was official sources that made these accounts of calls to Congress more newsworthy than the earlier talk show call-ins.)

ABC, for example, reported that Baird had a "rough time" on Capitol Hill and that she admitted knowing she was breaking the law. In a damning comment, the ABC reporter referred to her "unique defense" about acting as a mother. ABC said Baird was repeatedly "scolded," showing clips of Biden's comment about millions of Americans with one-fiftieth the income and Senator Specter pushing Baird to admit that she paid the Social Security taxes only because she had been nominated. ABC also reported Baird's admission that the only reason she paid the couple's taxes was her nomination. Still, her confirmation was "not thought to be in jeopardy." Similarly, CBS showed Biden, Thurmond, and Nader criticizing Baird; NBC showed Biden and Nader criticizing and Hatch praising her. CNN spoke of Baird's "admission and apology," showed her saying she made a mistake more as a mother, and referred to Biden's "verbal reprimand," but said confirmation "apparently remains on track."

On Wednesday, January 20—the day that Bill Clinton was to take his oath of office as president of the United States—most newspapers carried substantial, page 1 articles about the previous day's confirmation hearing. They referred to "tough" or "pointed" or "sharp" questioning, a "six-hour grilling," "scolding," and a "relentless focus" on Baird's INS troubles. These stories emphasized Baird's admission of a knowing violation and her apology; they quoted critical comments from various senators and noted the "deluge" of negative phone calls from constituents. Still, nearly all newspapers continued to predict that

Baird would be confirmed: "her nomination appeared to have survived" (she "showed her mettle" as a savvy lawyer—the *Boston Globe*); the lack of pledged votes "did not appear to undermine the likelihood of her eventual confirmation" *(New York Times);* the panel "still seemed inclined to vote for her" *(USA Today);* "likely to win confirmation" *(Chicago Tribune);* "likely to be approved" *(Wall Street Journal).* All these assessments were apparently drawn from the usual official sources. Only the *Los Angeles Times* and—more clearly—the *Washington Post* expressed doubt. The *Los Angeles Times* foresaw a "bumpier road" than expected, though confirmation still appeared likely. The *Washington Post* alertly (or hopefully) cited committee aides as saying that her confirmation—while still probable—"is not yet assured."

Continuing the trend of increasingly negative material creeping into the newspapers, however, Wednesday's minor news stories and opinion columns were decidedly mixed about Baird. Ellen Goodman and Anna Quindlen expressed empathy with the plight of hard-pressed working mothers; Mike Royko sarcastically dismissed the "scratching at minor legal points"; a *Wall Street Journal* editorial warned against liberal attacks on centrist doers and criticized the "awful" 1986 Simpson-Mazzoli law that had created this "Nanny Crime Wave." But a *Dallas Morning News* story noted that a Texas congressman had urged Clinton to withdraw the nomination; William Raspberry contrasted Baird's knowing violation of immigration rules with murky charges against Ron Brown; William Neikirk wrote that Clinton, knowing of Baird's offense, should not have nominated her; Debbie Price in the *Atlanta Constitution* cited Baird amid a long list of broken promises and ethical lapses by Clinton; and the *Washington Post*—Baird's most energetic and persistent media opponent—ran a devastating news story about Clinton's "Self-Inflicted Political Wound" at the Justice Department, describing career employees as "glum" and demoralized by the Baird disclosure; it quoted a prosecutor as calling Baird's actions "inexcusable." *USA Today* reported the poll showing that 51 percent of respondents considered her violation of the law a "major concern."

Opposition to Baird continued on talk radio and in phone calls to senators. Staff members later said that calls to Senator Paul Simon had been running twenty to one against Baird, and calls to Senator Carol Moseley-Braun (D-Ill.) ran forty-two to six against her (*Chicago Tribune*, Jan. 21, p. 18).

ABC, CBS, and NBC network news, full of inauguration stories, ran nothing on the Baird nomination that evening, but CNN mentioned Baird several times during the day. Her apology was briefly noted on *Daybreak* news; on later shows, Jody Powell mused that the Baird situation was a "minor thing" that should not prove to be a barrier; former senator Tim Worth predicted eighty-five or ninety Senate votes for her; and Wolf Blitzer said that, barring some unforeseen disclosure, Baird would still get confirmed. But most significant was a CNN special about government ethics. Bill Moyers, television commentator and former aide to Lyndon Johnson, remarked that, as a jaywalker himself, he would not want to be put in charge of the traffic cops; shouldn't Zoe Baird, who had knowingly and willingly violated an important law, withdraw her name from consideration as attorney general? Former congresswoman and prominent black Democrat Barbara Jordan replied, in her measured, forceful way:

> Bill, Zoe Baird should not be the attorney general of the United States of America. The attorney general is the chief law enforcement official of the country, and here you have a competent, savvy, knowledgeable person willfully violating the law. I believe that is a flaw which cannot be tolerated.

The elite consensus behind Baird was beginning to crumble.

ELITE RETREAT

During the course of Thursday, January 21, the last day before Baird's forced withdrawal, a sharp drop in official and media support for her became evident. As Baird again testified before the Judiciary Committee, public opposition continued to be expressed through radio talk shows, calls to congressmen, and two new national polls. Officials and the mainstream media finally began to back away from her.

That morning several news stories, while still calling confirmation likely, reported growing opposition. The *Chicago Tribune* saw a "rougher road ahead" for Baird and said that negative telephone calls had been flooding senators' offices. The *Dallas*

Morning News and *USA Today* quoted Barbara Jordan's appeal for Baird voluntarily to withdraw. The *Los Angeles Times* cast doubt on Baird's sworn denial that she knew about her neighborhood association's discrimination against a woman with ten adopted or foster black and Hispanic children. And the *Washington Post* hammered away, saying radio shows were "swamped" with calls about yuppie arrogance, and that Senate aides were startled by all the negative phone calls; it quoted Barbara Jordan, forecast that Gewirtz's testimony might imperil the nomination "even further," and ominously reported that Biden was "noncommittal" about whether Baird should withdraw.

Editorial commentary on this last day tilted heavily against Baird. An *Atlanta Constitution* editorial called for "hard scrutiny": "Baird is a flawed nominee. . . .The lone blot on her record is deeply troubling." It also ran four opinion columns with unfavorable references to Baird, and only one that was favorable. Four other newspapers *(Chicago Tribune, Dallas Morning News, Los Angeles Times, Washington Post)* each ran a negative opinion column (one of them likening Baird to Leona "only the little people pay taxes" Helmsley), with nothing positive. Some letters to the editor appeared in print: five negative and only one positive in the *Los Angeles Times;* two negative and one positive in *USA Today;* two negative in the *Washington Post.* The popular uproar had begun to find a voice on the editorial and op-ed pages of newspapers that previously had backed Baird.

Thursday's hearings went poorly for Baird, not because of new revelations but because senators, under pressure from their constituents, began to express opposition. Television, with a dramatically changed tone, gave a full account of Baird's decline. CNN previewed the hearing by asserting that calls for her to withdraw "appear to be increasing" and that senators' phone calls and faxes were running overwhelmingly against Baird. In the hearing, Senator Larry Pressler (R-S.D.) became the first to tell Baird he would have to vote against her. During a break in live coverage, CNN's legal expert called Baird's infraction "disqualifying." Around noon, Senator Herbert Kohl (D-Wis.) asked Baird whether it would be best for her to withdraw her nomination. During and after the hearing a number of senators, including Kassebaum (R-Kans.), Shelby (D-Ala.), Specter, Feinstein (D-Calif.) and Simpson made critical comments or urged Baird to withdraw.

The talk show blitz continued. According to host Joe Soucheray (KSTP, Minn.), Baird took up most of his air time all week; even though he wanted to move to another subject, "it was hot and heavy for two hours" on Thursday evening, when he got about fifty-five calls, most not favorable to Baird (*Los Angeles Times*, Jan. 22, 1993, p. 26).

The evening news shows aired clips of the senators' criticisms and reported that the nomination was in "deep trouble," in large part because of the pressure of public opinion. ABC showed Specter's and Feinstein's offices being flooded with calls from angry voters and said Feinstein's calls were running 1,500 to 33 against confirmation. Moreover, both CNN and ABC reported polls conducted that day (Thursday) in which large or "overwhelming" majorities of the American public opposed confirmation of Baird: by 63 percent to 23 percent (Gallup for CNN),[14] or 58 percent to 32 percent (ABC).[15] Seventy-three percent of the opponents told ABC the reason was mainly that she had employed the illegal immigrants.[16]

The drumbeat kept up on interview and talk shows. Larry King was startled by a caller who called the Baird appointment "horrendous." Lloyd Cutler's emergence to defend Baird on *Nightline* and *Crossfire* (where he took some heavy hits from Ralph Nader) did not stem the tide. A late CNN news show reported that the White House was backing away a bit from Baird. *Nightline* summed up the day: Baird was under fire from all sides, and the nomination was in deep trouble. It showed Senators Kassebaum and Simpson criticizing Baird, reported the 58–32 ABC poll, and said there was a "rising tide of sentiment" on the Judiciary Committee that Baird should take them off the hook by withdrawing; five Democratic senators and two Republicans had called for her to withdraw.

CNN quoted one Republican senator as quipping, "She's not in trouble, she's out." And so she was. Early the next morning, Baird's nomination was withdrawn. The popular uprising had prevailed.

CONCLUSION

Zoe Baird's hiring of illegal aliens for domestic work and her failure to pay Social Security taxes on them became widely known, in almost all important details, on January 14, the day the *New York Times* broke the story. Yet the major newspapers (including the *Times* itself) and television networks over the next five or six days reported little opposition to Baird and gave virtually no indication that a major scandal was threatening the incoming president's choice for attorney general. Nearly to the end, the great preponderance of news stories, relying heavily upon official sources, incorrectly predicted that confirmation of Baird would not be a problem.

There were several reasons for the mild reaction by public officials, including Democrats' loyalty to their new president (Biden, for example, apparently soldiered on despite grave reservations from the start [*Time*, Feb. 1, 1993, p. 33]), Republicans' feeling that Baird was the best they could get, and both parties' wariness about treating this milestone female nominee harshly, especially after what they had done to Anita Hill. The fact that the media mainly reported the views of official sources fits well with established findings and confirms what we have seen in previous chapters.[17]

For media figures as well as officials, however, the complacency about Baird's infractions also surely had something to do with their own economic-class and social-class positions. On the major media beats in New York and Washington, the days of hungry, working-class journalists were over. Media stars and U.S. senators moved together in high social circles, where illegal and untaxed domestic workers were not at all uncommon and seemed a minor peccadillo. In Howard Kurtz's revealing epilogue to the Baird affair, Leonard Downie Jr., executive editor of the *Washington Post,* acknowledged that many journalists in Washington were themselves in Baird's situation, which may have contributed to a sympathetic initial reaction. The *Wall Street Journal*'s Al Hunt agreed: "It may be that we live a life so unlike average citizens that we're really not very attuned to what they're thinking about."[18]

Questions of social class are often pushed beneath the surface of American politics, but in this case the class factor emerged with a vengeance, because many ordinary Americans could see that they disagreed sharply with Washington elites. They did *not* think it a minor matter that the proposed attorney general had violated laws that she would be called upon to enforce, particularly when her high family income would have permitted solutions beyond the reach of most working parents. As the early (Jan. 18–19) survey indicated, many citizens were seriously concerned about Baird's confirmation before officials or the mainstream media expressed such concern.

Calling radio talk shows and members of Congress, many people protested the nomination. This protest, further fueled by exposure to the hearings through live cable coverage and newsclips, and by increasingly critical editorials and opinion pieces, drove enough senators and other public figures into opposition so that the news media had to take notice and so that, rather quickly, the Baird nomination was withdrawn.

The causal impact of this popular uprising seems clear, both because of its priority in time and because of the extent to which officials and the media explicitly cited it in explaining their own and others' eventual defections from Baird. Moreover, the uprising seems to have been relatively spontaneous. Although various elites (Ralph Nader, trial lawyers, liberal activists) played a part in the early quiet grumbling about Baird and—along with a few editorials—probably helped provoke sharp questions in the Judiciary Committee hearings, and although those questions plus critical news stories and op-ed pieces—not just Baird's own unmediated testimony—helped spread public dissatisfaction, none of this elite activity had much to do with the early talk show call-ins or the early, widespread public concern. Practically none of it reached the public in time to do so. The bare facts of the case, as stated in bland news stories, seem to have done it. Even talk show hosts played a largely passive part. This was indeed a case of spontaneous combustion, not arson.

What should one make of it all? Not, we would suggest, that it was an entirely happy story of democratic triumph. Baird herself was subjected to a heavy dose of unexpected and (arguably) unfair pain and humiliation. The federal government lost the services of a highly skilled and intelligent person, for reasons that seemed to come out of the blue and to create a new hurdle for professional women seeking high office. (One wonders how many male nominees in past years, guilty of similar violations, had sailed through without question.) The whole unpleasant episode threatened to deter able people from considering public service. Moreover, some of the outrage over hiring illegal aliens—in California, for example, where immigration from

Mexico was arousing great anxiety—may have sprung from nativism or racism, rather than respect for the law or legitimate fear of economic competition.

Still, when all is said and done, the Baird episode was one in which ordinary U.S. citizens, reflecting the majority's values, insisted—over the resistance of most officials and media elites—upon applying certain not patently unreasonable legal and ethical standards to a major government appointment. In that sense it was, in fact, a victory for democracy, a demonstration that, under certain circumstances, unrepresentative surrogate deliberators can be overcome by direct, *populistic deliberation.*

What are the conditions under which such uprisings and populistic deliberation are likely to occur? We cannot be sure, but all the following conditions would seem to be necessary:

1. On some significant matter, officials and media elites hold in common, and act upon, preferences, beliefs, and/or values that are quite different from those of most ordinary citizens.

2. A large segment of the population becomes aware that elites are acting in this way.

3. Channels exist by which members of the public can express outrage.

The first condition, elite/mass divergence, may be met more often than we like to think. There are a number of large gaps, for example, between leaders and the public on foreign-policy issues.[19] Certain class-related domestic issues may also involve nearly monolithic consensus among elites and the media in opposition to majorities of the general public. On the other hand, some ostensible elite/public divergences and pseudopopulistic "firestorms" may be manufactured by narrow interests spreading misinformation. (This seems to have been the case, for example, with the 1980s campaigns against income tax withholding on interest income and against catastrophic health care coverage for the elderly.)[20]

The third condition, that channels for mass expression exist, tends to be met in all relatively open societies, but to varying extents. The "new" (or not so new)[21] media in the United States have probably opened up significant new channels by which ordinary people can more easily speak their minds and participate in deliberation, even when most officials and most owners, managers, and communicators in the traditional mass media disagree with them. Talk radio, despite the danger that unprincipled hosts may sometimes spread misinformation and manipulate their audiences, has at least the merit of providing microphones for spontaneous outbursts when they occur.

The second condition, public awareness, may be the most critical one. When is it likely to be met? If a major elite/mass divergence exists, members of the public cannot count on that fact being trumpeted by the professional policymakers and communicators upon whom they usually depend for political information. Ordinary people may be on their own. Perhaps the second condition tends to be satisfied, and populistic deliberation tends to occur, only when the facts are simple, clear, and uncontested, when they directly reveal elite/public differences, and when they are widely disseminated. That is, it may be met only when something apparently very simple and straightforward, like Baird's infractions, grabs public attention. More often, in messy and complicated matters like savings-and-loan regulation, tax breaks, deficits, international trade agreements, or Federal Reserve Board control of interest rates, ordinary citizens—if deprived of substantial elite competition—may be left at sea, unaware of policies that are harming them.

Popular uprisings of the Zoe Baird sort, then, are likely to be uncommon, and to leave untouched many large, important areas of public policy. Moreover, although we consider this definitely to be a case of deliberation (since the merits of a policy decision—a major appointment—were discussed), the *quality* of deliberation that uprisings can engender may be limited, more often involving expressions of anger than calm reflection, discussion, or research. The Baird incident, for example, while clearly establishing a new and not unreasonable ethical standard for prospective attorneys general of the United States, did not lead to much collective thinking through of broader issues about qualifications for public office (including possible sexist double standards), problems of day care, or dilemmas of immigration. We would not want to hold it up as an ideal case of public argument and reasoning among equal citizens.[22]

In short, populistic deliberation is a blunt instrument. Still, it is important that such an instrument exists for "enlarging the scope of conflict" and bringing about more democratic outcomes,[23] at least under certain limited circumstances.

That is the main lesson we draw from the Nannies case. It is also worth noting that it foreshadowed two problems that came to dog the first two years of the Clinton administration, undercutting President Clinton's popularity and contributing to low Democratic turnout in the 1994 congressional elections: repeated, unpleasant surprises about his nominees for various offices, and a sense that the administration—with many wealthy lawyers in the cabinet and a focus on issues like cutting deficits and freeing international trade—perhaps better represented high-income people like Baird than it did ordinary working-class Americans, who were worried about jobs and wages.[24]

NOTES

1. The following account rests mainly upon analysis of a comprehensive set of computer-retrieved or microfilmed stories mentioning Baird in ABC television network news, CNN, the *New York Times*, the *Wall Street Journal*, *USA Today*, the *Washington Post*, the *Atlanta Constitution*, the *Boston Globe*, the *Chicago Tribune*, the *Dallas Morning News*, and the *Los Angeles Times*. In addition, information on CBS and NBC television network news was drawn from the Vanderbilt summaries (Vanderbilt 1993). While obviously not constituting the whole of the U.S. media, these broadcasts and newspapers include many of the leading media organs in the country, with considerable geographical and ideological diversity. Our Nexis search used *Baird* as the main keyword and focused on dates from the announcement of the Baird nomination to shortly after her withdrawal.

2. It seems less likely that (as the *Wall Street Journal* later implied) the *Times* pursued the nanny story *because* of growing policy concerns, since the *Times* was very slow to voice any such concerns and since it treated the nanny story so gingerly. Quite possibly liberal sources at Justice, hoping to torpedo Baird, provided both stories. In a telephone interview (July 7, 1994), reporter Johnston did not seem eager to discuss such matters; he maintained that there was no connection between his policy-objection and nanny stories and "no sense of trying to time" the two. Nonetheless, their conjunction is interesting.

3. On indexing, see Bennett (1990).

4. Judging by the War case, the Riots case, and informal observation of hundreds of other instances over the years, this temporary disjuncture between the news and editorial pages at the *Times*—and the less marked disjuncture at the *Post*—was unusual. It resulted, we believe, from a confusing situation that came to pit editors' sympathies with the Democratic Party and the new President Clinton against their liberal

policy tendencies and their aspirations toward high ethical standards. In the end (sooner at the *Post* than at the *Times*) ethical and/or policy concerns won out over party on both the editorial and the news pages.

5. The following quotations and examples are largely taken from interviews with radio talk show hosts reported in Farrell (1993), Kurtz (1993), Reinhold (1993), and Shogren (1993).

6. Talk show callers apparently often reinforce, rather than contradict, the host and each other (Avery, Ellis, and Glover 1978, 14).

7. Telephone interview with Judy Jarvis (Nov. 4, 1994). Resonance—that is, viewer interest in and agreement with talk show hosts' suggestions—may be crucial to hosts' success at stimulating popular reactions. This is worthy of serious study. Viewers and listeners to particular shows may often be quite unrepresentative of the public as a whole and may (by self-selection) tend to have preexisting sympathy with hosts' views, but they are surely not blank slates upon which hosts can write at will.

8. Begala was quoted on "spontaneous combustion" in the *Atlanta Constitution*, February 1, 1993, A5. To our knowledge, neither Begala nor anyone else has suggested that Republicans or organized interest groups orchestrated these call-ins, as they have done in some other, pseudopopulistic, outpourings.

9. Tom Ferguson emphasizes the importance of trial lawyers, angry at Baird's espousal of "tort reform" and damage limitations, who had close links with public-interest attorneys like Nader and with the Democratic Party in many places including Barbara Jordan's Texas (personal communication, Aug. 9, 1994.) We agree that trial lawyers probably helped provoke the early (little-publicized) grumblings against Baird and the eventual defections by some Democratic senators and other officials; they may also have helped strengthen the Judiciary Committee questioning. But there is no evidence that they played a major part in stimulating the public outrage that proved central to Baird's undoing.

10. On various atypical characteristics of talk show callers, see Herbst (1995), Newhagen (1994), Armstrong and Rubin (1989), Bierig and Dimmick (1979), Avery, Ellis, and Glover (1978), and Turow (1974), but see also Hofstetter et al. (1994).

11. Survey evidence (Times Mirror 1993) indicates that talk show callers early in the Clinton administration tended to be a conservative, anti-Clinton "vocal minority."

12. The January 18–19 Gallup-CNN-*USA Today* question: "(Still thinking about the new Clinton administration, how much of a concern is each of the following to you—a major concern, a minor concern, or not a concern at all?) . . . That Bill Clinton's nominee for Attorney General, Zoe Baird, hired illegal aliens to work in her home in violation

of the law?" Responses: major concern, 51 percent; minor concern, 33 percent; not a concern, 15 percent; don't know/refused, 2 percent.

True, to some respondents this survey question probably introduced for the first time the fact of Baird's hiring illegals. But the results indicate that this bare fact was sufficient to provoke negative responses from many ordinary Americans who either already knew or were now told about it. Later, when knowledge of the fact became more widespread, large majorities of the public came to oppose the nomination.

13. The term elite refers to those with power, wealth, and high social status. Here we are concerned mostly with the subset of U.S. elites that was involved in mediated deliberation, especially federal officials and prominent journalists and commentators.

14. The January 21 Gallup-CNN question: "(As you may know, Zoe Baird and her husband have acknowledged they hired illegal immigrants in violation of the law to work in their home and take care of their child.) Do you think the U.S. (United States) Senate should vote to confirm Zoe Baird for the position of Attorney General, or not?" Responses: yes, 23 percent; no, 63 percent; it depends (volunteered), 2 percent; no opinion, 12 percent.

15. ABC poll, January 21, question 1: "As you may know, Bill Clinton has nominated Zoe Baird to serve as Attorney General. Baird has admitted she broke the law by hiring a couple who were illegal immigrants to work in her household and didn't pay Social Security taxes for them. She has paid a 29 hundred dollar fine, and apologized to the Senate Committee that's considering her nomination. Have you heard or read about the Baird nomination?" Question 2: "Do you think (Zoe) Baird should be confirmed by the Senate to serve as Attorney General, or not?" Responses: yes, 32 percent; no, 58 percent; no opinion, 10 percent.

Notice that this more balanced set of questions by ABC elicited only a little less negative reaction to Baird than did the one-sided Gallup-CNN question. (See the preceding note.)

16. The January 21 ABC follow-up question: "Do you feel that way (that Zoe Baird should not be confirmed by the Senate to serve as Attorney General) mainly because she employed the illegal immigrants (to work in her household and didn't pay Social Security taxes on them), or for some other reason?" Responses: because of immigrants, 73 percent; some other reason, 24 percent; no opinion 2 percent.

17. On the importance of officials as news sources, see Sigal (1973), Gans (1980), Hallin (1986), and Bennett (1990).

18. On the media being out of touch in the Nannies case for reasons of economic and social class, see Kurtz (1993; 1994, 300–302).

19. For examples of elite/mass gaps on foreign-policy issues, see Rielly (1987, 34–40; 1995, 38–40).

20. For a Congress-centered perspective on pseudopopulistic "fire-storms" in the 1980s, see Sinclair (1994, esp. 22).

21. Talk radio, though mushrooming in political importance, is not new; see Crittenden (1971), Munson (1993). Nor, of course, are letters or phone calls to public officials new, though they are now cheaper, eas-ier, and more susceptible to mass production.

22. A recent formulation of ideals for deliberation is Habermas (1992, esp. 446, 449–50). Peer and Herbst (1995) argue that talk radio can potentially provide for free, unstructured expression in "electronic salons."

23. Schattschneider (1960) argues that enlarging the scope of con-flict increases the power of citizens relative to organized interests.

24. On the multinational business base of the Clinton administra-tion, see Ferguson (1995, chap. 5 and 349–50). Woodward (1994) re-counts the high priority given to deficit cutting rather than economic stimulus.

FIVE

Conclusion: Successes and Failures of Mediated Deliberation

The War, Riots, and Nannies cases suggest—though of course they do not conclusively demonstrate—the existence of a number of patterns that may generally characterize public deliberation in the contemporary United States. The case studies, supplemented by the results of others' research and by less formal observations, can be summarized as follows.

PROFESSIONAL COMMUNICATORS

First, we have seen that *public deliberation is highly mediated.* In our populous, complex society, division of labor prevails. Most citizens get most of their political ideas and information through the mass media, and the voices speaking in and through the media are primarily those of *professional communicators,* whose jobs and livelihoods involve communicating with each other and the citizenry: public officials, researchers and publicists in academia and think tanks, reporters and journalists, television commentators, and the like.

When a political issue is debated in the mass media, only a tiny fraction of all the millions of U.S. citizens—perhaps only a few score of them—typically gain access to a nationwide audience. In the Riots case, for example, a thorough search of texts and transcripts from major media outlets produced the names of only seventy individuals who said something about Fitzwater's "1960s programs" charge. Virtually all of them were professional communicators—Bush administration officials, opposition Democrats, policy experts, journalists, television pundits. Much the same thing was true in the Nannies case: most media-transmitted discourse came from Senate Judiciary Committee and incoming Clinton administration officials, legal and other experts, reporters, and commentators.

Communications research has long established the primacy of *public officials* as key news sources.[1] The reasons for this primacy include officials' possession (sometimes exclusive control) of political information; the legitimacy and credibility conferred by their jobs; the convenience of access (to Washington, D.C., agencies and press conferences, for example) for "beat" reporters who can rely upon officials for quick, regular information handouts; and the need for reporters to cultivate good relations with these officials. But the central role of officials extends beyond news stories to op-ed columns and television commentary as well. As we saw with the Iraq war debate in the op-ed pages of the *New York Times,* even when speed and convenience of access is not a factor—even when there were more than two months in which to gather opinions from anyone, anywhere in the country—the media generally choose to stick closely to the views of public officials from the two major parties (along with in-tune former officials, advisers, and experts), so that public discourse in the mass media tends to "index," or reflect, only the range of debate between Republican and Democratic office holders.[2] When this range is restricted, so too, usually, is the range of public debate.

Another important kind of professional communicator is the *expert* on particular policy issues. Research has indicated that experts' views, as presented in the media, have a significant impact on public opinion: when experts speak in favor of a policy proposal, public opinion tends to move toward supporting that proposal.[3] The experts who show up in the media tend to be chosen for their accomplishments and credentials—recent publications on the subject, positions in leading universities or think tanks—but also for their accessibility to New York and Washington publications and television studios, and their eagerness to talk and their skill with a sound bite. Many have links and share viewpoints with government officials. Washington think tanks like the American Enterprise Institute, the Heritage Foundation, and the Brookings Institution make it their business to enter public discourse and are often successful at doing so; which ones are heard from most at a particular time tends to vary with the ideological currents of the day and the partisan control of government.[4]

Where do media-reported experts come from? How are they produced and credentialed? In part, through universities' training of graduate students and through the messy (and politically interesting) decisions in universities and elsewhere about what research to fund, what writings to publish, and whom to hire, promote, and tenure. In substantial part, also, experts emerge through the mysterious processes that establish, fund, and manage the private (usually nonprofit) research organizations and think tanks that do so well at getting their people and position papers into the media. Both universities and think tanks are undoubtedly influenced by social and political forces in the wider society, including the wealthy individuals and business corporations (and foundations they endow) who provide much of the money. Given the great importance of media-reported expertise in public debate, the political forces that govern the rise and fall of particular kinds of expertise deserve careful study.[5]

Different sets of experts are relevant to different policy problems. There was rather little overlap, for example, between the Council on Foreign Relations types who debated whether or not to go to war with Iraq, and the Urban Institute and Heritage Foundation experts who disputed the causes of the Los Angeles riots. Yet the importance of easy accessibility and quotable quotes encourages the emergence of some experts-on-everything. Political scientist Norman Ornstein, for example, was once known as the "king of quotes"; he appeared in hundreds of mass media stories each year.

Some of the most visible professional communicators have little or no expertise on substantive questions of public policy: the employees of media organizations (or freelancers) who work as *reporters, journalists, commentators, and television pundits.* These are the people who consult, quote, interview, and pontificate about the officials and experts; they are the ones whose words we read and whose heads we see talking much of the time on television. They include the leading national reporters for the *New York Times,* the *Washington Post,* the *Wall Street Journal,* and other elite newspapers; the anonymous editorial writers for these and other papers; and the reporters and anchorpersons for news shows on the major television networks. Perhaps most important, they include what Eric Alterman has called the "punditocracy": a relatively small group of commentators who write signed opinion columns in leading magazines or newspapers (often syndicated to many other papers), or who appear on radio or television discussion shows, or, in many cases, both write and talk.[6]

Research has indicated that media-reported commentators, like experts, have a substantial impact upon the policy preferences of the general public. When they take a stand, public opinion tends to move in the same direction.[7] Walter Lippmann once wielded a mighty pen.[8] When Walter Cronkite turned against the Vietnam War, many Americans listened. Thus the kind of people who become pundits, and the beliefs and values they hold, play an important part in political deliberation. Again, the forces that affect the shape of political commentary in the United States deserve investigation beyond what we can offer here.

DISTINCTIVE EDITORIAL STANDS BY DIFFERENT MEDIA

A second general theme from our cases is that, in their editorials and commentary, *different media outlets tend to take distinctive political stands*. Among newspapers, newsmagazines, and journals of opinion, these stands are usually manifested in unsigned editorials, which tend to be supported by regular and guest columns on op-ed pages and elsewhere. When television networks or programs take stands, they tend to be more muted and subtle, expressed through statements by employees, including discussion show hosts and participants, or through the media's choices of nonemployee commentators. These editorial positions tend to endure over time and may be related to the nature of particular audiences and to the ideological predispositions and/or economic interests of media owners and managers.[9]

It is no secret, for example, that the *Wall Street Journal*, a national newspaper published by the Dow Jones Corporation for the financial and business communities, generally takes quite conservative editorial stands on social and economic policy. Not only did the *Journal*'s editorial and op-ed pages fiercely attack the Great Society and defend Fitzwater in the Riots case and advocate "tort reform" and tolerance of illegal nannies in the Zoe Baird case; the *Journal*'s editorials and columns have a long history of favoring low (and nonprogressive) taxes, minimal government regulation, little or no downward redistribution of wealth or income, and the election to office of conservative Republicans.

Nor is it a secret that the *New York Times* and the *Washington Post* tend to take relatively liberal stands on these and other issues. Editorials and columns in both of them scornfully rejected Fitzwater's charge about the LA riots, strongly defending Great Society social programs; both eventually expressed unease that attorney general nominee Baird had committed the upper-class sin of hiring an illegal nanny. Both the *Times* and the *Post* regularly support government regulation of health, safety, the environment, and other matters, as well as public investment in education and infrastructure, provision of a social safety net for the most unfortunate Americans, and the election of Democrats. Both papers are dependable advocates for civil rights, civil liberties, and social tolerance. To be sure, their relative liberalism has its limits; both the *Times* and the *Post* are themselves big businesses, averse to unruly labor unions, high taxes, or any substantial redistribution of income or wealth. Still, on the spectrum of political views espoused by mainstream U.S. media, the *Times* and the *Post* fall near the left end.

The two newspapers are not identical. The *Post,* published in Washington, D.C., with its many federal government workers and its large African-American population, has an interest in selling papers to those audiences and has been quite attentive to them in its editorial stands. The *Post,* for example (as the Riots case indicated), is unusual among major U.S. dailies in regularly quoting African-American leaders and running columns by black commentators, and it pays particularly close attention to the ins and outs of domestic policy. The *New York Times,* on the other hand, located in a world business and financial center, is the leading internationalist media voice in the country, paying much attention to foreign affairs and devoting particularly strong editorial efforts to promoting free-trade agreements like the North American Free Trade Agreement (NAFTA) and the General Agreement on Tariffs and Trade (GATT). Owned by the Sulzberger family, the *Times* in recent decades has also been a strong backer of Israel (particularly of Labor, rather than Likud, governments and policies). The *Times'* Zionism may have been reflected in its strong editorial opposition to Saddam Hussein's Iraq, which was thought to pose a serious military threat to Israel.[10]

Other U.S. newspapers and magazines also tend to array themselves at various points on the ideological spectrum, according to their audiences' proclivities and their owners' ideological values and economic interests. As we saw, the *Washington Times*, linked with the Rev. Sun Yung Moon's Unification Church of Korea, is a particularly sharp voice on the far right, as are William Buckley's *National Review* (which has a bit more polish), the *American Spectator* (an enthusiastic digger into Clinton administration scandals), and the new *Standard* (which came onto the scene after the period of our cases, animated by William Kristol's neoconservatism and Rupert Murdoch's money). The left wing of U.S. media includes the austere, cheap-newspulp weekly *Nation* (long subsidized by wealthy liberal angels), the small, Wisconsin-based *Progressive*, the earnest *American Prospect,* and the lively, earthy *Mother Jones.* These publications inform and energize ideological activists and sometimes succeed in forcing new ideas and information into the mainstream media, but they cannot generally be said to play a large, direct part in public debate. (A prominent exception was the neoconservative *New Republic,* which became favorite reading material of the Reagan administration in the 1980s; the *Washington Times* and the *American Spectator* established similar links with congressional Republicans in the mid-1990s and won increased public attention.)

More centrist, mainstream publications also have distinctive editorial stances. As we saw, the moderately Republican *Chicago Tribune* and *Los Angeles Times*—located in major urban areas and concerned about social cohesion and economic viability in their cities—rebuked the Bush administration (mildly and briefly, to be sure) for the effort to blame the Los Angeles riots on Democrats' social programs; both called for serious government action to help the ghettos. On the foreign-policy front, both the *Tribune* and the *Los Angeles Times,* serving major centers of international commerce, have broken with their isolationist and protectionist pasts and now strongly advocate free trade and international activism. Many or most other U.S. newspapers and major newsmagazines *(Time, Newsweek, U.S. News and World Report)* tend to take similar stands—internationalist on foreign policy, receptive to some (limited) degree of government intervention in the domestic economy, and supportive of moderate Republicans.[11]

SLANTING NEWS

Our cases—plus informal observation and common sense—indicate that, in many newspapers and other media outlets, *political points of view* are not confined to editorial and op-ed pages but *pervade news stories* as well.[12] With the interesting exception of the *Wall Street Journal,*[13] the same political stands that are taken in editorials generally show up in the news.[14]

In the Riots case, for example, the *New York Times* and the *Washington Post* attacked Fitzwater and defended the Great Society in their news pages as well as editorials and opinion columns; so did the *Chicago Tribune,* whereas the *Washington Times* used a series of news stories to do just the opposite. In the early stages of the Nannies case, news stories as well as editorials in most mainstream media backed Baird, and later—under pressure—both turned against her.

The techniques for slanting news are known, at least in principle, to most savvy readers and viewers, but they sometimes slide past our conscious defenses—and presumably affect our thinking—when we are not alert. The whole repertoire of techniques (conscious or unconscious)[15] was on particularly clear display in the Riots case.

One of the most important techniques, and probably one of the most effective because of its unobtrusiveness, is *to control the prominence* with which a story is pursued and displayed. ("Give me the headlines and you can have the editorials," the saying goes.) As a glance at different newspapers published on any given day will indicate, editors have considerable leeway to decide what's news, what will get a big play, and what will be minimized or ignored altogether.[16] Those decisions can be motivated, consciously or unconsciously, by political considerations. Prominent placement in a newspaper, especially on page 1 above the fold, promotes substantial reader attention. So do big headlines, backup stories, sidebars, and continuations on the front and inside pages, and follow-up stories over a number of days—or, on television, long and repeated stories and placement as the top news of the day.[17] High prominence can be given to stories that are politically congenial to media editors and owners, and withheld from those that are not.

We saw how the relatively liberal *New York Times* and *Washington Post* used the technique of prominent coverage to help turn Fitzwater's comments into a big, continuing national story.[18] On the other hand, newspapers that were generally sympathetic to the Bush administration, like the *Chicago Tribune* and the *Los Angeles Times,* quickly dropped the subject. In the Nannies case, the *New York Times'* initial enthusiasm for Baird led it to ignore policy-related objections to her until the illegal-alien revelation was in its hands. Another example, among many: in May 1995, when peace talks between Israel and the Palestinians were threatened by an Israeli decision to confiscate 130 acres of Arab land in Jerusalem in order to build Jewish housing, the United States cast a veto in the UN Security Council (its first veto in five years), in order to block a resolution criticizing Israel that was supported by all fourteen other council members. The *New York Times,* which regularly gives international events page 1 prominence and big headlines, consigned this story to minor treatment on page 4, presumably in order to minimize embarrassment to Israel and the Clinton administration.[19]

A second important technique—which again can slip by the unwary reader or viewer—is *to solicit, select, and shape quotations* around which a news story is built. The canons of objectivity dictate that when opinions are expressed, they are supposed to be quoted from or attributed to some named—or at least described—source. But reporters and editors have a great deal of freedom to decide whom to seek out for quotes, which of their words to use (or twist), and which quotations actually to include in the story. Each of these decisions can, consciously or unconsciously, be used to support editorial policy. The officials, experts, and others who are solicited for opinions may be those who tend to agree with the paper's editorial policy. The quotations used—in or out of context, with or without accidental or purposeful distortions (and there is many a slip between thought and sound bite)—may be those that advance the political views of media reporters, editors, and owners.

Again the Riots case provides a number of good examples. The conservative *Washington Times'* front-page news story, subheadlined "'Great Society' Not So Great, Critics Say," was particularly noteworthy for its selection of quotations: starkly anti–Great Society quotes from conservative think tanks like the Heritage Foundation and the Hoover Institution, a few criticisms from carefully chosen Democrats, and out-of-context critical phrases from Great Society supporters (May 10, 1992). The *Washington Post* and the *New York Times*, on the other hand—while making more of a show of evenhandedness in their quotes—rounded up a galaxy of experts to support federal social programs. And they unearthed or provoked particularly devastating quotations against Fitzwater, like the one from the anonymous Republican official who joked that next the Bush White House would be blaming the savings-and-loan crisis on Woodrow Wilson (*New York Times*, May 7, 1992, p. 22).

Another technique is *to choose which facts to report* so as to advance editorial purposes. Uncertainty over what is true and what false gives media considerable leeway to report varying realities; so does selection among multitudes of relatively uncontested facts. The political beliefs and values of editors and reporters are bound to influence which facts they see as newsworthy and as illustrating the true meaning of events.

In reporting Fitzwater's charge about 1960s programs, for example, the *Times* and the *Post* noted various factual aspects of the political context—that President Bush was running poorly in the polls, that Fitzwater himself had just attacked Clinton for playing politics with the riots and now admitted that it was "a political year," that Bush had not fought hard for his own domestic agenda. These were relevant chiefly because the *Times* and the *Post* interpreted the story in political "horse race" terms, as a tactical move to gain partisan advantage. The (few) supporters of Fitzwater, on the other hand, like the *Washington Times*, filled their news stories with facts or anecdotes concerning waste, inefficiency, and failure in social programs.

A closely related technique is *to frame the meaning of news stories* so as to further media editors' and owners' political purposes. Framing is a subtle and delicate art that can be accomplished in a variety of ways.[20] The purpose is to make the reader or viewer see things the medium's (or a reporter's or source's) way: to see Fitzwater's comments, for example, as a crude partisan attack, or as a serious analysis of government failure. Framing is often accomplished at the very outset of a news story, in an opening interpretive sentence or sentences, organizing the first facts and quotations that are presented.

Still another technique for slanting news, the least subtle one—which, in fact, the rules of objectivity once supposedly banned from mainstream newspapers—is *to use overtly evaluative words and statements.* *Time* magazine long ago pioneered the deployment of colorful adjectives and adverbs (e.g., the "great statesman," Chiang Kai-shek of nationalist China;[21] *mossback* conservative Republicans, in contrast to *new* Eisenhower Republicans) and punchy verbs (bad guys tended to *slink, slouch, whimper,* or *bluster*; good guys would *stride* or *electrify the crowd*) in order to make its editorial points. More recently even the sober "gray lady" of journalism, the *New York Times,* has livened itself up—and sometimes abandoned the pretense of objectivity—by using openly evaluative language.

Since readers and viewers can rather easily detect blatantly loaded language and may be annoyed by it, however, the most important evaluative words and statements in news and interpretive stories are probably the quietest, blandest, most inconspicuous ones. A particularly clever example in the Riots case was the *New York Times* piece on "Decoding . . . Fitzwater . . . ," which argued in a matter-of-fact tone that of course Fitzwater could not have been referring "in purely factual terms" to actual social-welfare programs (May 6, 1992, p. 24). The clear implication: Fitzwater's charge was false.

Evaluation in news stories is, of course, unavoidable. Even the most self-consciously neutral language carries evaluations; this is most obvious when criminal acts (e.g, genocide), or news sources' pernicious lies, are reported in deadpan style without any hint of disapproval—thus tending to condone them. Most language that seems nonevaluative seems so only because it reflects values that are so widely shared we are unconscious of them. One might argue that the decline of "objectivity" and the rise of openly evaluative language actually help audiences, by unmasking evaluations that were always present but disguised. Still, some kinds of news slant can have seriously negative consequences.

MEDIA AS POLITICAL ACTORS

One of the most important implications of the War, Riots, and Nannies cases (a point not often discussed in the communications literature) is that *certain media outlets*—especially newspapers and magazines, but sometimes also televisions programs and networks—do not merely reflect the social and political forces around them; instead, they *actively work to shape political discourse to their own purposes.*[22]

The War and Riots cases were particularly striking in this regard. The *New York Times* constructed its editorial and op-ed discussions of whether or not the United States should go to war with Iraq in such a way that its own editorial position was buttressed by many regular and guest columns and was symmetrically flanked on both sides (the slightly more dovish and the slightly more hawkish) by almost precisely equal numbers of dissents. This had the effect of making the *Times'* own position seem middle-of-the-road, centrist, moderate, reasonable—even though it was considerably less open to negotiation and compromise than most U.S. citizens were, and even though many significant kinds of experts, organizations, and viewpoints were excluded from the debate.

Similarly, in the Riots case, several newspapers (most notably the relatively liberal *New York Times* and *Washington Post* and the conservative *Washington Times*) deployed their news stories, editorials, regular columns, and guest columns, all in a coordinated fashion, to make and emphasize the points they wanted to make. The *Times* and *Post* were particularly notable for the way in which they built up Fitzwater's remarks with prominent coverage, criticized them strongly in news stories, editorials, and columns, and hammered away at the subject for more than two weeks. The *Washington Times* coordinated its news and editorial pages in a counterattack.[23]

The importance of media outlets as political actors, however, rests largely upon the extent to which they agree with each other and all promote or oppose the *same* political ideas, either independently or because some media influence others and shape the overall course of debate. If they do not agree, if there is vigorous competition and substantial diversity of viewpoints among media, then one could argue that coordinated political action by each individual outlet makes little difference; citizens can sort through contending positions and the "marketplace of ideas" can work well.

But there are indications that the influence of certain leading media outlets, and/or agreement among most major mainstream media, may sometimes be sufficient to affect public discourse as a whole. The *New York Times* and *Washington Post*, in particular, seem to have a great deal of influence over other media. The reporters and editors of other newspapers and magazines read the *Times* and *Post;* so do those who assign and write television news stories or put together television discussion shows. In the Riots case, we saw that many other media picked up the story that the *Times* and the *Post* emphasized, used similar arguments and facts, and ran similar commentaries. Influence in such cases is difficult to pin down with certainty, but the sequence of events, in which the *Times* and *Post* early on wrote lengthy stories and editorials, and other media outlets followed later, using similar or identical language, strongly suggests a causal connection.[24]

The influence of the *Times* is likely to be especially great in the area of foreign policy, where it is widely seen as the preeminent, most authoritative daily organ. Thus, in the War case, it is possible that the *Times'* decisions about what guests to feature on its op-ed pages and what to say in its editorials and regular columns significantly affected what other media outlets perceived as the legitimate range of debate. To be sure, the observed uniformity among media could also have occurred because other media independently used similar criteria (deferring heavily to government officials, former officials, and a limited set of experts). But either way, the mainstream mass media, either under the leadership of the *Times* or acting individually under common principles, behaved as political actors, made political choices, and restricted the public debate about war with Iraq.

OUT-OF-TOUCH MEDIA

The War case, and even more so the Nannies case, indicate that the *mainstream news media*—and the officials and experts upon whom they rely—*are sometimes out of touch with the values of ordinary citizens.* When this happens, professional communicators may take public deliberation in directions that are uncongenial and unhelpful to the citizenry as a whole.

In the case of the Iraq war, whatever the merits of the *Times'* own position (sanctions first, but war if necessary; no compromise), that position and the debate constructed around it largely ignored ordinary citizens' desires—desires that were made clear in a number of opinion surveys—for negotiations and compromise. The Nannies case displayed an even sharper discrepancy between media elites and ordinary citizens. Although most citizens who learned of Zoe Baird's illegal hiring of domestic workers were quite unhappy about it, few officials or media elites were much troubled. Most supported Baird's confirmation until very late in the game, and nearly all predicted confirmation right up to the brink of Baird's withdrawal. This stance resulted in part from the media's reliance upon key officials in the Senate Judiciary Committee and the incoming administration, who had reasons of party loyalty or ideology for sticking by Baird; but officials and media figures alike seem also to have been affected by their own class positions. Affluent officials and journalists were accustomed to seeing their friends, if not themselves, disregard immigration laws and Social Security tax requirements.

An important question is how often and under what circumstances such elite-mass gaps occur. We have suggested that they are not so uncommon as one might wish. In foreign policy, average Americans have often disagreed markedly with public officials, experts, and media figures about a wide range of issues. For example, ordinary citizens have tended to be considerably less enthusiastic than foreign-policy elites about the use of force abroad, about economic or (especially) military aid or arms sales, and about free-trade agreements. The average American is much more concerned than foreign-policy elites about jobs and income at home.[25] On some issues these gaps are so great that public discourse, as articulated by officials, experts, and journalists, may be quite distant from the values and concerns of ordinary citizens. (This may have been true, for example, of the 1992–93 NAFTA debate, in which few voices other than that of the billionaire populist Ross Perot were heard warning about the "giant sucking sound" of U.S. jobs moving south to Mexico.)[26] Particularly when the leaders of both major parties, under the banner of "bipartisan foreign policy," agree on something that most citizens tend to oppose (e.g., the post-NAFTA bailout of investors in Mexico in 1995), public deliberation in the mass media tends to be severely constricted.

Similarly, there are indications of substantial elite-mass gaps in values concerning certain kinds of domestic economic policies. Ordinary citizens, at least when they are aware of what is at stake,[27] tend to favor full employment, expansionist monetary policy, and low interest rates, whereas political, business, and media elites tend to prefer to fight inflation, even at the cost of severe budget cutting, tight money, economic slowdown, and high joblessness.[28] Again, the problem for public deliberation is most severe when officials of both parties and most mainstream media take positions that are similar to each other and opposed to the public. An especially painful example of two-party collusion is the savings-and-loan disaster of the 1980s, in which some $200 billion—nearly one thousand dollars for each woman, man, and child in the country—was lost, but neither the Republican nor the Democratic Party (both entangled with big savings-and-loan campaign contributors) warned of trouble, acted to prevent it, or raised a fuss afterward. The media, too, were largely silent.[29]

As was emphasized in chapter 1, out-of-touch elites and media can be very damaging to public deliberation, because they may prevent a competitive marketplace for ideas from functioning. If elites do *not* compete by offering diverse ideas that connect with ordinary citizens, we cannot expect citizens to sort through media-provided information and arrive at well-informed policy preferences. If media and other elites stand together against the public, for whatever reason—elites' own class positions, or two-party collusion to protect themselves and their investors, or monopoly government control of foreign-policy information—there is a serious danger that the public will be misled and that democracy will not work properly.

POPULISTIC UPRISINGS, REAL AND SIMULATED

As the Nannies case indicates, when the mainstream media are out of touch with the citizenry, *a populistic uprising can sometimes use other communications channels* to get around and overcome them. When virtually all mainstream newspapers and television programs downplayed or ignored the revelations about Zoe Baird's employment of illegal aliens, an outpouring of angry voices on talk radio and phone calls to senators provoked sharper questions from the Judiciary Committee, turned around politicians' and media's stands, and led to Baird's withdrawal.

Talk radio is not the only alternative medium with this kind of subversive potential. Storms can brew up on the Internet or via fax machines; challenging ideas can percolate out to the public through underground newspapers, small journals of opinion, or even the thousands of tiny (often one-person) "'zines" that can be located through listings in magazine racks and bookstores.[30] The information system in the United States is highly permeable, and advances in technology promise to make it even more so. There definitely exist channels that can be used for populistic uprisings.

Still, as we argued in chapter 4, genuine popular uprisings of the Zoe Baird sort are not likely to occur often. Communications channels are available, and substantial elite-mass differences often occur, but one crucial ingredient is frequently lacking: even when public policy and discourse go against the values of the citizenry, citizens may often remain unaware of the conflict. That is to say, rather often when (or *because*) the media monolithically ignore a problem or take a position contrary to the interests (that is, to the hypothetical fully informed preferences) of the public, most citizens may be tranquilized or persuaded into going along. This can happen when politicians of both major parties, Republicans and Democrats alike, agree on what to suppress or what to advocate; or when the government holds a near monopoly of information, as in foreign-policy crises; or when the class interests of most officials, experts, and media owners and employees lead them to values opposed to those of average citizens. Such elite-mass discrepancies are particularly likely to go unperceived by the citizenry if time is short (as in some foreign-policy crises), or if issues seem minor and have low visibility (as in many special tax preferences), or if the issues are complex and hard to understand (as in macro-economic policy or the savings-and-loan disaster).

Indeed, genuine uprisings of the Zoe Baird sort may be quite unusual; they may occur only when the bare facts of the case are quite simple, uncontested, and understandable and are widely communicated by the mainstream media, so that millions of people receive information that is sufficient to provoke rebellion. In the Baird case, as opinion survey data indicate, the barest facts were sufficient to kindle outrage in most citizens.

Have these conditions been met in other cases? Have other genuine popular uprisings occurred? There do seem to have been other cases in which widespread public anger, expressed on talk radio and elsewhere, was sparked by simple facts that did not trouble most political and media elites. The large (and long-postponed) congressional pay raise of 1989, for example, which struck most elite observers—including this author—as merely making up for inflation and as helping to protect public servants from temptation by private money, greatly upset many ordinary citizens who were under severe economic pressure and felt unhappy with government.[31] Similarly, the House of Representatives' check-writing scandal of 1991–92, which elites (again including the present author) and the mainstream media mostly considered a trivial matter of free overdraft protection that cost no public money, nonetheless aroused considerable public anger and contributed to the defeat of a number of incumbent representatives in 1992.[32] In both these cases it is possible that talk radio performed the same function it did in the Zoe Baird case, allowing ordinary citizens to break through and overpower a mainstream media consensus based on different values.

Still, it would be unwise to jump to that conclusion without a thorough investigation. There are indications that organized interest groups, partisan politicians, and ideologically motivated talk show hosts may sometimes succeed in spreading false or misleading information to the public or a faction of it, creating pseudopopulistic revolts and "firestorms" of phone calls and faxes to Congress that actually work against most citizens' interests. This appears to have been true, for example, of the misleading campaign that exaggerated prospective Medicare fee increases (which would have affected only the most affluent elderly) and overturned an expansion of catastrophic health insurance in 1989; this campaign was orchestrated by an organization that apparently represented high-income elderly people.[33] Likewise, the 1982–83 "populistic" campaign of cards and letters to repeal tax withholding on interest and dividends—hardly a concern of Joe Sixpack—was energized by inflammatory rhetoric ("the government is going to loot your savings") that banks mailed to their customers.[34] In the congressional pay raise and House banking cases, much of the agitation may have originated with Newt Gingrich and other House Republicans (and with conservative talk show hosts) eager to displace the Democratic congressional majority. Several of the uprisings against early Clinton administration appointments and policies also bore the marks of partisan organization, with Republican officials faxing charges and arguments to sympathetic talk show hosts like Rush Limbaugh, who stirred up their listeners—sometimes on the basis of misinformation.[35]

The test of genuineness in a popular uprising is not a total lack of elite involvement, which is virtually inconceivable and not necessarily desirable; political information useful to an insurgent public might properly come from anywhere. The test, instead, is whether protests voiced through alternative media correspond to the values of most ordinary Americans, as they come to be expressed (or would be expressed) in accurately informed preferences.[36] The *whole* public is relevant, not just some noisy faction; ordinarily this can be judged only through survey research, using scientific, representative samples. And the uprising has to represent the real values of the public, not manipulated preferences based on systematic misinformation.

The Zoe Baird uprising clearly passes this test; so—but with some qualification[37]—might the congressional pay raise and House banking cases. But some other cases clearly would not.

SUCCESSFUL AND NOT SO SUCCESSFUL DELIBERATION

This book has largely focused on hazards and deficiencies in mediated deliberation, but it is important not to ignore the positive side. Indeed, the War, Riots, and Nannies cases themselves can be read as embodying substantial deliberative success. The populistic uprising over Zoe Baird established a not wholly unreasonable new standard for U.S. attorneys general; finger pointing about blame for the Los Angeles riots led to some reasoned discussion of the nature and effects of social-welfare programs (at least those benefiting the middle class); and even the rather limited *New York Times* op-ed debate about war with Iraq aired some important facts and ideas, especially concerning the *Times'* preferred policy of economic sanctions.

In any case, we should not forget our starting point: somehow or other, the U.S. public has managed to form generally sensible collective policy preferences, which usually respond in reasonable ways to events and objective realities.[38] This suggests that mediated deliberation, despite its flaws, must be largely successful.

How is that possible? As was discussed in chapter 1, we believe that mediated deliberation can work well if decentralization and division of labor take the proper form. A division of labor concerning the production and communication of ideas—which is unavoidable in a large, complex society—can also be effective and efficient, so long as there is sufficient public-oriented *competition* and *diversity* among the ideas and information that specialists produce and distribute to the public. So long as useful information is available and is publicized by at least some highly visible cue-givers and opinion leaders, ordinary citizens have the skills and motivation to sort through contending views and pick (or reshape) those that make sense and are helpful.[39] The finding that there is a "rational public," with generally sensible and responsive collective policy preferences, indicates that enough diversity and competition among ideas is provided so that mediated deliberation usually works fairly well.

In order for mediated deliberation to be successful, it is probably *not* necessary, therefore, that the political views expressed in the mass media meet hard-to-define, and difficult-or-impossible-to-enforce, standards of perfect balance or absence of bias. (As we asked in connection with the War case, *which* views deserve to be balanced, around *what* ideal midpoint? From what ideal kind of representativeness should bias or deviation be measured? And how could such standards be imposed upon any single medium, let alone the mass media as a whole, without grossly infringing upon freedom of speech?)

Instead, classical liberals like John Stuart Mill and Oliver

Wendell Holmes may have been correct: the marketplace of ideas actually works reasonably well, most of the time, so long as there is sufficient competition and diversity in the information system. Competition is a powerful force; true and useful ideas, once they are enunciated somewhere, have a way of spreading, willy-nilly, everywhere. Ideas that originate in relatively obscure places—in research organizations, tiny 'zines, or small-circulation journals—diffuse through word of mouth, the Internet, talk radio, and the like, and often leak into the mainstream media.[40] That is, the same permeability and multiplicity of communications channels that can (as in the Nannies case) permit a popular uprising against out-of-touch mainstream media more often serve to keep those media reasonably in touch with, and responsive to, the public.

The onward rush of electronic communications technology will presumably increase the diversity of available ideas and the speed and ease with which they fly about and compete with each other.[41] True, e-mail, the Internet, and other computer-based means of communications (indeed, even faxes) are not at all equally accessible to all citizens; their maldistribution adds to the already great political advantages of people with high incomes, who can afford to buy personal computers and other equipment. But access to such means of communications shows at least some signs of spreading beyond the most affluent, for example through computer terminals at libraries. Talk radio, too, has tended to favor an unrepresentative set of hosts and listeners (with politicians in some cases probably taking it too seriously as a gauge of overall public opinion), but there are indications of growing diversity and competition in talk radio and of increasingly sophisticated reactions to it.[42] And, of course, it is possible that defects of any one communication channel may be compensated for by other channels.

Often a crucial factor in competition among ideas is the passage of time, especially in cases that start out with relevant information under monopoly control. To put it in the language of economics, even if correct information and useful ideas tend to prevail over falsehoods in equilibrium, it may take a long time to reach that equilibrium. For example, officials' misrepresentations about the "unprovoked" 1964 North Vietnamese attack on U.S. destroyers in the Gulf of Tonkin, and mythology about "nation building" and "light at the end of the tunnel" in Vietnam, dominated the mainstream media for years, until the Tet Offensive of 1968 fractured the unified government line and the media's adherence to it.[43] In a later and more skeptical era, much of the misleading propaganda that dominated media coverage of the 1991 war with Iraq was rather quickly exposed and discredited after the war was over.[44] The lesson is double edged. On the one hand, the truth tends to come out eventually, and it probably now comes out more and more quickly, as levels of education and skepticism rise and as communications technologies expand. On the other hand, the public often has to make decisions before the full truth is known, as in the 1964 election (when President Johnson was portrayed as the peace candidate) and the 1972 election (when President Nixon was widely seen as innocent of Watergate crimes). In cases of delayed deliberation, election outcomes and policy decisions—even decisions to go to war—can be affected by false or misleading discourse.

Because of the frequently crucial role of the passage of time in working out competition among ideas, a full understanding of mediated deliberation and a firm assessment of its successes and failures will require investigation over much lengthier time periods than those involved in the War, Riots, and Nannies cases. It will also necessitate examining the whole range of communications media through which political ideas can flow, including television and film entertainment, cartoons, commercial and political advertising, radio and television talk and discussion shows, and electronic networks, as well as print media of every sort, from little-known 'zines to blaring supermarket tabloids, and from obscure tracts to glossy magazines. Moreover, a satisfactory understanding of mediated deliberation must take account of how ideas and information are produced in the first place by scholars, universities, think tanks, and others, and how and by whom those ideas and information are launched into public discourse.[45] To follow even one small policy idea carefully, through all relevant communications pathways, would be no slight undertaking.

WHAT TO DO?

What about the negative side, the hazards of mediated deliberation. What should one do about them?

For individual media consumers (students, say, or just plain citizens), the answer is easy: be wary and shop around. Whenever you read or see political material, exercise skepticism. Figure out motivations and ideologies in the newspaper, magazine, or television show you are looking at; watch for its editorial thrust and for slants in the news or information it presents. What stories are made prominent? Why? What is ignored? Who is quoted, and why? What evaluative material is slipped in? Try to read between the lines, spotting what the reporter did *not* say, and try to dig out obscure but important bits that contradict the main story line. (Even those who gnash their teeth at the *New York Times'* opinion pushing often find gems buried in the inside pages of that newspaper, which, on a daily basis, presents more political news than any other medium.)

Wariness and skepticism alone are not enough, however; you also need exposure to alternative ideas. Before you make up your mind on what's right or whom to trust, open yourself to a diversity of media voices. Do not stop with CNN or the evening news; drop by a discussion show and a special or two, and surf over, at least occasionally, to PBS and C-Span. Maybe even try talk radio. (Check out more than one host, though; different hosts often live in different worlds.) If you have computer access, wander through the Net—but be warned about the lack of quality control; the "facts" you encounter may be fantasies. Don't depend too much on your local paper, with its predigested wire service coverage; stop by a library or newsstand and take a look at elite newspapers like the *Wall Street Journal,* the *New York Times,* and the *Washington Post.* Leaf through newsmagazines and journals of opinion. Even if you are very busy, occasional browsing can turn up valuable tidbits of political information and help you decide which media (if any) to follow regularly.

Most important: expose yourself to a real diversity of ideas. Make an effort, from time to time, to glance at media you generally disagree with. Many a liberal has been amazed at what can be gleaned from the news pages of the *Wall Street Journal;* many a conservative has been startled by investigative reporting in *Mother Jones* or the *Nation.* Especially when an official government line is dominating most of the media (e.g., during foreign-policy crises), or when the Republican and Democratic Parties are both agreeing on something (e.g., hushing up joint misdeeds), try to find dissenting journals or commentators who may offer a disturbing or a refreshing thought.

For citizens who want to influence policy, advice on what to do is also fairly simple: take the time and energy to identify and mobilize those who agree with you; find media that will spread your message—mainstream media if you can break into them, alternative media if you cannot—and pester politicians to respond. For most citizens, the inside game of Washington lobbying, where big campaign money and large organizations have the most clout, is usually frustrating, but the "outside strategy" of mobilizing activists and the general public can stir up voters and make politicians listen. If the citizenry as a whole once learns about and accepts your ideas, policy in harmony with those ideas is likely to follow.

The "what to do?" question is harder to answer for those who would like to improve the overall system of public deliberation in the United States. Anything as vast and complicated as our whole information system is not easy to change. Features of mediated deliberation that you dislike may reflect such fundamental factors as corporate ownership of the media, the me-too two-party system, the weakness of the U.S. labor movement,[46] the great political strength of business corporations, the absence of a mobilizing social-democratic party, and even the pressures of international economic competition[47]—none of which will vanish tomorrow.

On a more modest, practical level, heckling the media and news sources about gross slants or excesses may help. Campaign "truth squads" can sometimes improve public discourse.[48] Media watchdogs like the professionally oriented *Columbia Journalism Review*, the liberal Fair and Accuracy in Reporting (which publishes *Extra!*), and the conservative Accuracy in Media at least make the media more self-conscious about slanted news and probably curb some of the most blatant excesses. A 1994 story in *Extra!* on Limbaugh's errors and misstatements, for example, may have helped prod him into tempering some of his wilder assertions.[49]

It is especially important, given our analysis of competition among ideas, to encourage and increase media diversity. You might help out money-losing, nonmainstream journals, for example, by contributing, working, publicizing, or at least subscribing to them,[50] and by making sure that neighbors, coworkers, fellow group members, and public officials know about them.

It is also worth working hard to break up monopoly or duopoly control over political information and ideas wherever it appears: in "bipartisan" foreign policy, for example, the ideology of which deserves critical examination; or in alleged national-security imperatives that sometimes keep Americans ignorant of what is being done in their name, while adversaries or victims abroad know all too well; or in two-party collusion to please major investors.

Measures to decrease the influence of money on public officials (e.g., by requiring full disclosure, limiting contributions, and substituting public for private financing of campaigns) would help make deliberation by those officials more responsive to ordinary citizens—that is, more democratic.[51]

It may be impossible any time soon to end altogether the power that money, organization, and government authority have over ideas, but that power can be limited. To force elites to face articulate opposition and to make their cases in the open, in front of the citizenry, is surely within the realm of political feasibility.

NOTES

1. Seminal works on the importance of officials as news sources include Sigal (1973), Gans (1980), and Hallin (1986). See also Cook (1989).

2. For evidence that a small set of interconnected, official-centered commentators dominates television discussion shows as well as news programs, see Reese, Grant, and Danielian (1994). On media indexing of official views, see Bennett (1990).

3. Findings on the impact of media-reported experts' statements upon the collective policy preferences of the public are reported in Page, Shapiro, and Dempsey (1987) and in Page and Shapiro (1992, 343, 347–48).

4. Soley (1992) discusses the partisan and ideological affiliations of media-quoted experts. Domhoff (1983, chap. 4) locates experts within a corporate-dominated "policy-planning network" that plans policy alternatives and shapes opinion to support them.

5. Antonio Gramsci (1971 [1929–35]) persuasively argued that intellectuals (including the academics and other experts discussed here) generally perform the function of ideologically supporting the established powers in society. See Gramsci, "The Concept of Ideology" and

"The Formation of the Intellectuals," in Mattelart and Siegelaub (1979, 99–105).

6. Alterman (1992) describes the "punditocracy"; see also Reese, Grant, and Danielian (1994).

7. The impact of commentators on public opinion is shown in Page, Shapiro, and Dempsey (1987) and in Page and Shapiro (1992, 343–47).

8. On the amazing career of Walter Lippmann, see Steel (1980).

9. As noted in chapters 2 and 3, media owners' influence upon their outlets' editorial stands need not be heavy-handed, interventionist (though a number of such interventions have been reported—see Bagdikian 1992), or even conscious; it can result from owners hiring and retaining like-minded editors, perhaps giving them occasional guidance, and from those editors tending to hire, retain, promote, and encourage like-minded editorial writers and commentators.

Devereux (1993) discusses the partisan and ideological stands of a number of newspapers and the likely economic and ideological reasons for them. D. Chomsky (1995b) explores the mechanisms by which some media owners control the contents of their publications.

10. Zionism has always been a sensitive issue for the Jewish-owned *Times*, which initially opposed the establishment of Israel and for many years tried to avoid the appearance of too many Jewish-looking bylines. See Talese (1970, 71–74, 111–14).

11. On the predominance of free-trade internationalist media in the United States, and their role as gatekeepers in presidential election politics, see Devereux (1996).

12. As previously noted, professional journalists and communications researchers tend to be skeptical of links between editorial stands and news slants, or of any influence by media owners upon news content, and little study has been directed at such matters. Once again: correspondence between news and editorial points of view can occur without any conspiracy, without any contact, without any breach of the "wall of separation" between the news and editorial departments. All that is needed is a tendency (even an unconscious tendency) for owners and publishers to hire and retain like-minded editors in both realms, with or without subsequently intervening in what they do. Sometimes, no doubt, news stories influence subsequent editorials (as may have happened in the *New York Times'* switch against Zoe Baird), or vice versa.

13. The unusually frequent disjunctions between the news and editorial pages of the *Wall Street Journal* do not, of course, mean that the *Journal*'s news stories are somehow miraculously value free (an impossibility); it merely means that they tend to reflect somewhat different values than the editorials do. A possible reason: the editorial and op-ed

pages may feel free to indulge even the crankiest and most far-out no-
tions of its quite conservative business and financial audience (this
makes readers feel good and does little harm), but businesspeople and
financiers, no matter what their personal views, need to rely on the
news pages to learn what is happening and what most Americans are
actually thinking.

14. Rowse (1957), on the Nixon and Stevenson "funds," is one of the
few existing analyses of how multiple newspapers' varying slants on a
single news story have tended to correspond with their editorial stands.
Our Riots case contributes additional evidence on this point.

15. Our language about media outlets' "techniques" or "purposes"
in slanting news in harmony with their editorial positions is just convenient shorthand. There is not necessarily any conscious action by a
single, unitary actor. Media organizations, like most organizations, act
through the often unconscious and only loosely coordinated behavior
of many autonomous-feeling individuals. Nonetheless, through various mechanisms previously discussed, publications and television programs often come to have a unity of editorial thrust, and a set of ways to
express it, that are best described in this unitary-actor language.

16. On the process of deciding—or constructing—what's news, see
Tuchman (1978) and Gans (1980).

17. In other words, the media have important "agenda setting" effects upon what people think about. See McCombs and Shaw (1972),
Iyengar and Kinder (1987).

18. The *Times* and *Post* are described as only "relatively" liberal, despite their positions near the most liberal end of the political spectrum
among mainstream media, because, in relation to the opinions of the
U.S. public, their positions are generally centrist. As best one can judge,
they tend to stand near the center of public opinion on many issues
(safety nets, middle-class social-welfare policies, the environment,
health and safety regulation, women's issues), to be more liberal on a
few issues (freedom of speech, rights of the accused, social tolerance),
and to be more conservative than the average citizen on some (progressive taxation, job creation, rights of labor). Simply to call these newspapers "liberal" would be misleading.

19. *New York Times*, May 19, 1995, 4.

An amusing example of selective coverage that varied among media
outlets: when the *New Republic* in 1995 revealed that Senator Phil
Gramm of Texas (who, as a candidate for the Republican nomination
for president, was actively courting social conservatives) had years ago
invested in a soft-porn movie, the tabloid *New York Post* and *New York
Daily News* headlined "Porno-Gramm" and "Pol Put His Bucks into
Porn." Several mainstream newspapers *(Washington Post, Wall Street*

Journal, Los Angeles Times) took at least brief notice. But the *New York Times*, which had published 66 stories dealing with Paula Jones's allegations of past sexual misbehavior by then-governor Bill Clinton, did not—in the first few days—make a single mention of the Gramm story. The *Washington Times*, which had run more than a 130 Paula Jones stories, gave Gramm a supportive headline: "Gramm Denies Prurient Motivation for Blind Investment in R-rated film." Gary Trudeau's *Doonesbury* comic strip spent a week mocking Gramm. See the *New Yorker*, June 5, 1995, 31–32.

20. On framing, see Tuchman (1978), Gitlin (1980), Pan and Kosicki (1993), Entman (1993), and (for the effects of media frames on audience reactions) Iyengar (1991).

21. A still-interesting example of owners' and editors' (unusually overt) control over news reporting is Henry Luce's and *Time* editor Whittaker Chambers's persistent reworking of Theodore White's World War II reports from China, in order to make Chiang Kai-shek and his nationalists (by then thoroughly unpopular among the Chinese people) look like heroes. See Griffith (1995, esp. chaps. 6, 7).

22. Again, our language concerning media outlets' activity and "purposes" is convenient shorthand. The decentralized actions of many different media employees often achieve sufficient coordination (not perfect coordination, of course—principal-agent problems, if nothing else, would prevent that) so that their joint output, their publications or programs, can appropriately be described as purposeful and goal directed. As we have discussed, this coordination may result from a variety of possible causal mechanisms, including owners' and managers' ultimate power to hire and fire their employees, as well, perhaps, as occasional interventions into employees' decisions. Thus certain media may act as if they were unitary, purposeful actors pursuing goals corresponding with their owners' ideological values or economic interests.

23. These judgments are based upon analysis of what the newspapers printed. Evidence on exactly how the news stories, editorials, and columns came to be coordinated, what mechanisms led to their common political thrust, must come from different kinds of research: from participant observation, study of statements in memoirs and interviews, or (most reliably) analysis of internal memos and other documents that can be obtained only through archival research. See Devereux (1993a) and Chomsky (1995b).

24. An old but telling example of the *Times'* influence over other media is Timothy Crouse's vignette of journalists from the Associated Press, United Press International, CBS, NBC, ABC, and the *Baltimore Sun* all peering over the shoulder of the *Times* reporter (R. W. Apple) as

he typed his interpretation of the 1972 Iowa Democratic caucus. The next day, practically all the media followed the *Times'* line about a "surprisingly strong" showing by George McGovern. See Crouse (1973, 84–85).

25. See Rielly (1995, 38–40), and the elite/mass "Gap" chapters of earlier quadrennial reports from the Chicago Council on Foreign Relations.

26. On NAFTA and the 1992 election, see Ferguson (1995, chap. 6).

27. The issue here concerns elite-mass differences in values, and in actual or hypothetical preferences held on the basis of full information, not necessarily in *expressed preferences*, which may be different due to manipulation by distorted public discourse. Evidence on these matters, like the more sweeping notion of false consciousness, is inherently difficult to gather, but that does not lessen the possibility that opinions are sometimes manipulated or decrease the importance of such possible manipulation.

28. See, for example, *Time* magazine's issue of May 22, 1995 (featuring a meat cleaver on the cover), which enthused about budget cutting at the same time that it reported (p. 33) survey data showing large public majorities opposed to cutting any major program other than defense. (*Time* fudged the interpretation of its own data, overemphasizing people's willingness to "sacrifice.")

29. Kurtz (1994, chap. 3) gives a good account of the media's (non)coverage of the savings-and-loan debacle.

30. *Factsheet 5*, available in many bookstores, regularly carries reviews of hundreds of 'zines and tells how to obtain them. See, for example, Jeff Kelly's *Temp Slave!* which describes and protests the bleak lot of temporary workers, a topic long ignored in the mainstream media.

On other means of communication used by societally marginal groups, see Herbst (1994) and Fraser's (1992) analysis of multiple, competing public spheres.

31. See Federal Communications Commission (FCC) commissioner James Quello's complaint that radio talk show hosts and disk jockeys aroused public opposition to Congress's (and his own) pay raise, in *Broadcasting*, May 8, 1989, 42–44, and March 13, 1989.

32. See Viles (1992).

33. On the catastrophic health insurance case, see *Congressional Quarterly Almanac*, 1989, 150.

34. On the case of withholding dividend and interest taxes, see Sinclair (1989, 167–68).

35. On errors and misstatements by Rush Limbaugh, see Fairness and Accuracy in Reporting (1994).

Another bit of pseudopopulism: the *Wall Street Journal*, policing minor right-wing pressures against the ratification of GATT in 1994, found that much of the noise came from activists financed by textile chieftain Roger Milliken, and that the thousands of calls that Senator Bob Dole received from Kansas against the World Trade Organization were mostly placed by one group of one hundred volunteers who logged some sixteen thousand phone calls to Dole's office during the summer. ("That's us!" the organizer gleefully told the *Journal* [Nov. 23, 1994, A16].)

36. This correspondence between the contents of alternative media and the values of ordinary citizens is related to the medium/audience *resonance* discussed in the Nannies case.

37. The qualification: if citizens had been fully aware of comparable private-industry salaries and of the corruption-avoidance argument, or of the small and non-taxpayer-borne costs of House check kiting, they might not have been so angry as surveys showed them to be. It is very difficult to judge such hypotheticals.

38. On the "rationality" of the public, and its ability to form sensible collective policy preferences—sometimes despite propaganda or nonsense from the government and media—see Page and Shapiro (1992).

39. On audiences as active constructors of meaning, see Graber (1984) and Gamson (1992).

The benign effects of selection among competing ideas and information are argued in J. S. Mill (1947 [1859]), Holmes (1919), and Page and Shapiro (1992, 362–66, 390–91), among others.

40. *The New York Times,* for example, now periodically reports what's happening on the Internet and on talk radio, and it has even taken account of the existence of 'zines. See Zane (1995).

41. The increasing diversity of political information made possible by increases in types and channels of communication, however, may be offset in whole or in part by continuing increases in the concentration of media ownership, so that a few huge corporations control most major types of media (see Bagdikian 1992).

42. Talk radio, once seemingly the indisputable province of Rush Limbaugh and "angry white male" conservatives, has apparently seen an upswing of competing liberal and left-populist hosts like Jim Hightower, Tom Leykis, and Chuck Harder; see the *Nation,* April 10, 1995, 482–92. And public officials, initially stunned by talk show–stimulated outpourings of calls and letters, may have started to discount pseudopopulistic "firestorms" resulting from unrepresentative, organized campaigns, just as they earlier learned to take with a grain of salt "spontaneous" mass mailings of identical postcards or letters.

43. On the media's long-standing deference to officials concerning U.S. policy in Vietnam, see Hallin (1986).

44. On coverage of the Iraq war, see Bennett and Paletz (1994), Kellner (1992), Chomsky (1992), and Cumings (1992). O'Loughlin, Mayer, and Greenberg (1994, esp. chap. 4) detail a number of unpleasant effects of the war.

45. Gandy (1982), for example, explores the production and distribution of political ideas in terms of "information subsidies," many of which come from corporations.

46. On the marked paucity of labor, as opposed to business, interest group spokespersons on television, see Danielian and Page (1994).

47. For an argument that increased capital mobility and lowered costs of international transactions have greatly increased the political power of capital as opposed to labor, not only in the United States but throughout the world, see Winters (1995). If workers in all advanced industrial countries are under pressure from international wage competition, if the political power of business is at a peak, and if government policies are constrained by competitive pressures (e.g., if wage or tax increases to help workers would lead to capital flight), then the public discourse of officials and other professional communicators, as well as public policy itself, is likely to reflect these facts and not be very responsive to ordinary workers and citizens.

48. Kathleen Hall Jamieson's crusade against Willie Horton–style dirty politics, for example, seems to have helped mute "attack ads" in 1992; see Jamieson (1992).

49. See Fairness and Accuracy in Reporting (1994). Limbaugh apparently felt obliged to respond, and he eventually submitted a thirty-seven-page rebuttal that *Extra!* demolished in turn (*Extra! Update,* December 1994, 3).

50. Journals of opinion generally cost much more to produce than they take in from subscriptions, ads, and newsstand sales. According to Schulman (1995, 11), during the 1990–93 period four leading conservative journals received more than $2.7 million in subsidies from foundations (Olin, Carthage, Scaife, Bradley, Smith-Richardson, Coors), while four leading progressive journals received (from MacArthur, Schumann, Diamond) less than $270,000—one-tenth as much.

51. On the reform of campaign finance, see Ferguson (1995, conclusion).

Alterman, Eric. 1992. *Sound and Fury: The Washington Punditocracy and the Collapse of American Politics.* New York: HarperCollins.

Armstrong, Cameron B., and Alan M. Rubin. 1989. Talk Radio as Interpersonal Communication. *Journal of Communication* 39(2): 84–94.

Austen-Smith, David. 1990. Information Transmission in Debate. *American Journal of Political Science* 34(1): 124–52.

Avery, Robert K., Donald G. Ellis, and Thomas W. Glover. 1978. Patterns of Communication on Talk Radio. *Journal of Broadcasting* 22(1): 5–17.

Bagdikian, Ben H. 1992. *The Media Monopoly.* 4th. ed. Boston: Beacon.

Barber, Benjamin. 1984. *Strong Democracy: Participatory Politics for a New Age.* Berkeley and Los Angeles: University of California Press.

Bennett, W. Lance. 1988. *News: The Politics of Illusion.* 2d. ed. New York: Longman.

———. 1990. Toward a Theory of Press-State Relations in the United States. *Journal of Communication* 40(2): 103–25.

Bennett, W. Lance, and David L. Paletz, eds. 1994. *Taken by Storm: The Media, Public Opinion, and U.S. Foreign Policy in the Gulf War.* Chicago: University of Chicago Press.

Bessette, Joseph M. 1978. Deliberation in Congress: A Preliminary Investigation. Ph.D. dissertation, University of Chicago.

———. 1994. *The Mild Voice of Reason: Deliberative Democracy and American National Government.* Chicago: University of Chicago Press.

Bierig, Jeffrey, and John Dimmick. 1979. The Late Night Radio Talk Show as Interpersonal Communication. *Journalism Quarterly* 56: 92–96.

Boyte, Harry. 1995. Beyond Deliberation: Citizenship as Public Work.

Paper presented to the PEGS conference on Civic Competence, Washington, D.C., Feb. 10–11.

Braestrup, Peter. 1976. *Big Story: How the American Press and Television Reported and Interpreted the Crisis of Tet 1968 in Vietnam and Washington.* 2 vols. Boulder, Colo.: Westview.

Brody, Richard A. 1991. *Assessing the President: The Media, Elite Opinion, and Public Support.* Stanford, Calif.: Stanford University Press.

Bryan, Frank. 1995. Direct Democracy and Civic Competence: The Case of Town Meeting. Paper presented to the PEGS conference on Civic Competence, Washington, D.C., Feb. 10–11.

Calhoun, Craig, ed. 1992. *Habermas and the Public Sphere.* Cambridge, Mass.: MIT Press.

Carey, James W. 1989. *Communication as Culture: Essays on Media and Society.* Boston: Unwin Hyman.

Carroll, Vincent. 1991. The Scarcity of Anti-War Editorial Voices. *Washington Journalism Review,* January–February, 14.

Chomsky, Daniel. 1995a. Constructing the Cold War. Ph.D. dissertation, Northwestern University.

———. 1995b. One Degree Left of Center: The Mechanisms of Management Control. Paper presented at Northwestern University, June 15.

Chomsky, Noam. 1992. *Deterring Democracy.* New York: Farrar, Straus and Giroux.

Cohen, Bernard C. 1963. *The Press and Foreign Policy.* Princeton, N.J.: Princeton University Press.

Cook, Timothy. 1989. *Making Laws and Making News: Media Strategies in the U.S. House of Representatives.* Washington, D.C.: Brookings.

Crittenden, J. 1971. Democratic Functions of the Open Mike Radio Forum. *Public Opinion Quarterly* 35: 200–210.

Crosby, Ned. 1995. A Request for Help. Paper presented to the PEGS conference on Civic Competence, Washington, D.C., Feb. 10–11.

Crouse, Timothy. 1973. *The Boys on the Bus.* New York: Ballantine.

Cumings, Bruce. 1992. *War and Television.* London: Verso.

Dahl, Robert A. 1956. *A Preface to Democratic Theory.* Chicago: University of Chicago Press.

———. 1989. *Democracy and Its Critics.* New Haven: Yale University Press.

Danelian, Lucig H., and Benjamin I. Page. 1994. The Heavenly

Chorus: Interest Group Voices on TV News. *American Journal of Political Science* 38(4): 1056–78.

Davis, Otto A., Melvin J. Hinich, and Peter C. Ordeshook. 1970. An Expository Development of a Mathematical Model of the Electoral Process. *American Political Science Review* 64: 426–48

Deese, David A., ed. 1994. *The New Politics of American Foreign Policy.* New York: St. Martin's.

Derthick, Martha, and Paul J. Quirk. 1985. *The Politics of Deregulation.* Washington, D.C.: Brookings.

Devereux, Erik August. 1993a. The Partisan Press Revisited: Newspapers and Politics in the United States, 1964–1968. Ph.D. dissertation, University of Texas, Austin.

———. 1993b. The Press and the Los Angeles Unrest of 1992. Working paper 93-37, Heinz School of Public Policy, Carnegie Mellon University.

———. 1996. *Guarding the Gates.* Forthcoming.

Dewey, John. 1954 [1927]. *The Public and Its Problems.* Athens, Ohio: Swallow Press.

Domhoff, G. William. 1983. *Who Rules America Now?* Englewood Cliffs, N.J.: Prentice-Hall.

Dorman, William A., and Mansour Farhang. 1987. *The U.S. Press and Iran: Foreign Policy and the Journalism of Deference.* Berkeley and Los Angeles: University of California Press.

Dorman, William A., and Steven Livingston. 1994. News and Historical Content: The Establishing Phase of the Persian Gulf Policy Debate. In *Taken by Storm*, ed. W. Lance Bennett and David L. Paletz, 63–81. Chicago: University of Chicago Press.

Downs, Anthony. 1957. *An Economic Theory of Democracy.* New York: Harper.

Edelman, Murray. 1988. *Constructing the Political Spectacle.* Chicago: University of Chicago Press.

Entman, Robert M. 1989. *Democracy without Citizens: Media and the Decay of American Politics.* New York: Oxford University Press.

———. 1991. Framing U.S. Coverage of International News: Contrasts in Narratives of the KAL and Iran Air Incidents. *Journal of Communication* 41(4): 6–27.

———. 1993. Framing: Toward Clarification of a Fractured Paradigm. *Journal of Communication* 43(4): 51–58.

Entman, Robert M., and Benjamin I. Page. 1994. News before the

Storm: The Iraq War Debate and the Limits to Media Independence. In *Taken by Storm: The Media, Public Opinion, and U.S. Foreign Policy in the Gulf War,* ed. W. Lance Bennett and David L. Paletz, 82–101. Chicago: University of Chicago Press.

Entman, Robert M., and Andrew Rojecki. 1993. Freezing Out the Public: Elite and Media Framing of the U.S. Anti-Nuclear Movement. *Political Communication* 10: 155–73.

Entman, Robert M., and Steven S. Wildman. 1992. Reconciling Economic and Non-Economic Perspectives on Media Policy: Transcending the "Marketplace of Ideas." *Journal of Communication* 42(1): 5–19.

Fairness and Accuracy in Reporting. 1994. The Way Things Aren't: Rush Limbaugh Debates Reality. *Extra!* July–August, 10–17.

Farrell, John Aloysius. 1993. Baird: Reminder of Populist Outrage. *Boston Globe,* January 23, 1.

Ferejohn, John A., and James H. Kuklinski, eds. 1990. *Information and Democratic Processes.* Urbana: University of Illinois Press.

Ferguson, Thomas. 1995. *Golden Rule: The Investment Theory of Party Competition and the Logic of Money-Driven Political Systems.* Chicago: University of Chicago Press.

Ferguson, Thomas, and Joel Rogers. 1986. *Right Turn: The Decline of the Democrats and the Future of American Politics.* New York: Farrar, Straus and Giroux.

Fishkin, James S. 1991. *Democracy and Deliberation: New Directions for Democratic Reform.* New Haven: Yale University Press.

Fitzwater, Marlin. 1995. *Call the Briefing.* New York: Random House.

Ford, Daniel. 1984. *The Cult of the Atom: The Secret Papers of the Atomic Energy Commission.* New York: Simon and Schuster.

Fraser, Nancy. 1992. Rethinking the Public Sphere: A Contribution to the Critique of Actually Existing Democracy. In *Habermas and the Public Sphere,* ed. Craig Calhoun, 109–42. Cambridge, Mass.: MIT Press.

Freedman, Lawrence, and Efraim Karsh. 1993. *The Gulf Conflict 1990–91: Diplomacy and War in the New World Order.* Princeton, N.J.: Princeton University Press.

Gamson, William. 1992. *Talking Politics.* New York: Cambridge University Press.

Gandy, Oscar H., Jr. 1982. *Beyond Agenda Setting: Information Subsidies and Public Policy.* Norwood, N.J.: Ablex.

Gans, Herbert J. 1980. *Deciding What's News: A Study of CBS Evening News, NBC Nightly News, Newsweek, and Time*. New York: Random House.

Garment, Suzanne. 1991. *Scandal: The Crisis of Mistrust in American Politics*. New York: Random.

Garnham, Nicholas. 1992. The Media and the Public Sphere. In *Habermas and the Public Sphere*, ed. Craig Calhoun, 359–76. Cambridge, Mass.: MIT Press.

Geiger, Jack. 1994. Bomb Now, Die Later: The Consequences of Infrastructure Destruction for Iraqi Civilians in the Gulf War. In *War and Its Consequences*, ed. John O'Loughlin, Tom Mayer, and Edward S. Greenberg, 51–58. New York: HarperCollins.

Gervasi, Tom. 1986. *The Myth of Soviet Military Supremacy*. New York: Harper.

Gitlin, Todd. 1980. *The Whole World Is Watching: Mass Media in the Making and Unmaking of the New Left*. Berkeley and Los Angeles: University of California Press.

Gooding-Williams, Robert, ed. 1993. *Reading Rodney King, Reading Urban Uprising*. New York: Routledge.

Goulden, Joseph C. 1969. *Truth Is the First Casualty*. Chicago: Rand McNally.

Graber, Doris. 1984. *Processing the News: How People Tame the Information Tide*. New York: Longman.

Gramsci, Antonio. 1971 [1929–35]. *Selections from the Prison Notebooks*. Ed. and trans. Quintin Hoare and Geoffrey Nowell Smith. New York: International Publishers.

Griffith, Thomas. 1995. *Harry and Teddy*. New York: Random House.

Habermas, Jürgen. 1974 [1964]. The Public Sphere: An Encyclopedia Article. *New German Critique* 3: 49–55.

———. 1989 [1962]. *The Structural Transformation of the Public Sphere*. Trans. Thomas Burger. Cambridge, Mass.: MIT Press.

———. 1992. Further Reflections on the Public Sphere. Trans. Thomas Burger. In *Habermas and the Public Sphere*, ed. Craig Calhoun, 421–61. Cambridge, Mass.: MIT Press.

Hallin, Daniel C. 1986. *The "Uncensored War": The Media and Vietnam*. New York: Oxford University Press.

Hamilton, Alexander, James Madison, and John Jay. 1961 [1787–88]. *The Federalist Papers*. Ed. Clinton Rossiter. New York: New American Library.

Herbst, Susan. 1993. *Numbered Voices: How Opinion Polling Has Shaped American Politics.* Chicago: University of Chicago Press.

———. 1994. *Politics at the Margin: Historical Studies of Public Expression Outside the Mainstream.* New York: Cambridge University Press.

———. 1995. On Electronic Public Space: Talk Shows in Theoretical Perspective. *Political Communication,* forthcoming.

Herman, Edward S., and Noam Chomsky. 1988. *Manufacturing Consent: The Political Economy of the Mass Media.* New York: Pantheon.

Higgins, C. S., and P. D. Moss. 1982. *Sounds Real: Radio in Everyday Life.* New York: University of Queensland Press.

Hofstetter, C. Richard, Mark C. Donovan, Melville R. Klauber, Alexandra Cole, Carolyn J. Huie, and Toshiyui Yuasa. 1994. Political Talk Radio: A Stereotype Reconsidered. *Political Research Quarterly* 47: 467–79.

Holmes, Oliver Wendell. 1919. Opinion in *Abrams v. U.S.* 250 U.S. 616, 630.

Iyengar, Shanto. 1991. *Is Anyone Responsible? How Television Frames Political Issues.* Chicago: University of Chicago Press.

Iyengar, Shanto, and Donald R. Kinder. 1987. *News That Matters: Television and American Opinion.* Chicago: University of Chicago Press.

Jamieson, Kathleen Hall. 1992. *Dirty Politics: Deception, Distraction, and Democracy.* New York: Oxford University Press.

Jarvis, Judy. 1993. Perspectives on Zoe Baird: To Main Street, It's a Crime; Judiciary Committee, Transition Team, and the Nominee Herself Still Don't Get It; Nobody Is Above the Law. *Los Angeles Times,* January 22, B7.

Jordan, Donald L. 1993. Newspaper Effects on Policy Preferences. *Public Opinion Quarterly* 57: 191–204.

Kellner, Douglas. 1992. *The Persian Gulf TV War.* Boulder, Colo.: Westview.

Kelman, Steven. 1987. *Making Public Policy: A Hopeful View of American Government.* New York: Basic.

Kurtz, Howard. 1992. Television's Political Impressions in Riots' Aftermath. *Washington Post,* May 7, A30.

———. 1993. Talk Radio's Early Word on Zoe Baird: Listeners' "Nannygate" Reactions Signaled Trouble for Nominee. *Washington Post,* January 23, B1.

———. 1994. *Media Circus: The Trouble with America's Newspapers.* New York: Random.

Lasch, Christopher. 1990. The Lost Art of Political Argument. *Harpers,* September, 17–22.

Lichter, S. Robert, Stanley Rothman, and L. S. Lichter. 1986. *The Media Elite.* Bethesda, Md.: Adler and Adler.

Lippman, Walter. 1965 [1922]. *Public Opinion.* New York: Free Press.

Maass, Arthur. 1983. *Congress and the Common Good.* New York: Basic.

Mansbridge, Jane J. 1980. *Beyond Adversary Democracy.* New York: Basic.

———. 1986. *Why We Lost the ERA.* Chicago: University of Chicago Press.

Marchetti, Victor, and John D. Marks. 1984. *The CIA and the Cult of Intelligence.* Rev. ed. New York: Dell.

Mattelart, Armand, and Seth Siegelaub, eds. 1979. *Communication and the Class Struggle.* Vol. 1. New York: International General.

Mayer, Jane, and Jill Abramson. 1994. *Strange Justice.* Boston: Houghton-Mifflin.

McCombs, Maxwell E., and Donald L. Shaw. 1972. The Agenda-Setting Function of Mass Media. *Public Opinion Quarterly* 36: 176–87.

McCubbins, Mathew D., and Arthur Lupia. 1995. *Can Democracy Work?* Typescript, University of California, San Diego, July.

McKelvey, Richard D., and Peter C. Ordeshook. 1986. Information, Electoral Equilibria, and the Democratic Ideal. *Journal of Politics* 48: 909–37.

McQuail, Denis. 1992. *Media Performance: Mass Communication and the Public Interest.* Beverly Hills, Calif.: Sage.

Mill, John Stuart. 1947 [1859]. *On Liberty.* New York: Appleton-Century-Crofts.

———. 1958 [1861]. *Considerations on Representative Government.* Indianapolis, Ind.: Bobbs-Merrill.

Monoson, S. Sara. 1994. Frank Speech, Democracy, and Philosophy: Plato's Debt to a Democratic Strategy of Civic Discourse. In *Athenian Political Thought and the Reconstruction of American Democracy,* ed. J. Peter Euben, John R. Wallach, and Josiah Ober, 172–97. Ithaca, N.Y.: Cornell University Press.

———. 1996. *Plato and Athenian Democracy.* Princeton, N.J.: Princeton University Press, forthcoming.

Mueller, John. 1994. *Policy and Opinion in the Gulf War.* Chicago: University of Chicago Press.

Muir, William K., Jr. 1982. *Legislature: California's School for Politics.* Chicago: University of Chicago Press.

Munson, W. 1993. *All Talk: The Talk Show in Media Culture.* Philadelphia: University of Pennsylvania Press.

Nacos, Brigitte Lebens. 1990. *The Press, Presidents, and Crises.* New York: Columbia University Press.

Newhagen, John E. 1994. Self-Efficacy and Call-in Political Television Show Use. *Communication Research* 21(3): 366–79.

O'Loughlin, John, Tom Mayer, and Edward S. Greenberg, eds. 1994. *War and Its Consequences: Lessons from the Persian Gulf Conflict.* New York: HarperCollins.

Page, Benjamin I., and Robert Y. Shapiro. 1984. Presidents as Opinion Leaders: Some New Evidence. *Policy Studies Journal* 12: 649–51.

———. 1992. *The Rational Public: Fifty Years of Trends in Americans' Policy Preferences.* Chicago: University of Chicago Press.

Page, Benjamin I., Robert Y. Shapiro, and Glenn R. Dempsey. 1987. What Moves Public Opinion? *American Political Science Review* 81: 23–43.

Pan, Zhongdang, and Gerald M. Kosicki. 1993. Framing Analysis: An Approach to News Discourse. *Political Communication* 10(1): 55–75.

Parenti, Michael. 1993. *Inventing Reality: The Politics of News Media.* 2d. ed. New York: St. Martin's.

Patterson, Thomas E. 1993. *Out of Order.* New York: Knopf.

Peer, Limor, and Susan Herbst. 1995. Talk Shows as Electronic Salons: The Nature of Discourse in a Rational Public Sphere. Paper presented at the annual meeting of American Political Science Association, Chicago, Aug. 30–Sept. 3.

Peters, John Durham. 1993. Distrust of Representation: Habermas on the Public Sphere. *Media, Culture, and Society* 15: 541–71.

Powlick, Philip J. 1990. The American Foreign Policy Process and the Public. Ph.D. diss, University of Pittsburgh.

Reese, Stephen D., August Grant, and Lucig H. Danielian. 1994. The Structure of News Sources on Television: A Network Analysis of *CBS News, Nightline, MacNeill-Lehrer,* and *This Week with David Brinkley. Journal of Communication* 44(2): 84–107.

Reinhold, Robert. 1993. Settling In: An Angry Public; Fueled by Radio and TV, Outcry Became Uproar. *New York Times,* January 23, 9.

Rielly, John E., ed. 1987. *American Public Opinion and U.S. Foreign Policy 1987.* Chicago: Chicago Council on Foreign Relations.

———, ed. 1995. *American Public Opinion and U.S. Foreign Policy 1995.* Chicago: Chicago Council on Foreign Relations.

Rojecki, Andrew. 1994. Arms Control Movements and the Media: From the Cold War to the Nuclear Freeze. Ph.D. dissertation, Northwestern University.

Rowse, Arthur Edward. 1957. *Slanted News: A Case Study of the Nixon and Stevenson Fund Stories.* Boston: Beacon.

Russett, Bruce. 1990. *Controlling the Sword: The Democratic Governance of Foreign Policy.* Cambridge, Mass.: Harvard University Press.

Sabato, Larry. 1991. *Feeding Frenzy.* New York: Free Press.

Schattschneider, E. E. 1960. *The Semisovereign People: A Realist's View of Democracy in America.* New York: Holt.

Schulman, Beth. 1995. Foundations for a Movement: How the Right Wing Subsidizes Its Press. *Extra!* March–April, 11–12.

Schumpeter, Joseph A. 1950. *Capitalism, Socialism, and Democracy.* 3d. ed. New York: Harper and Row.

Shawcross, William. 1992. *Murdoch.* New York: Simon and Schuster.

Shogren, Elizabeth. 1993. Calls against Baird Flooding Talk Shows. *Los Angeles Times,* January 22, A26.

Sifry, Micah L., and Christopher Cerf, eds. 1991. *The Gulf War Reader: History, Documents, Opinions.* New York: Random House.

Sigal, Leon V. 1973. *Reporters and Officials: The Organization and Politics of Newsmaking.* Lexington, Mass.: D. C. Heath.

Sinclair, Barbara. 1989. *The Transformation of the U.S. Senate.* Baltimore, Md.: Johns Hopkins University Press.

———. 1994. Congress, the Public, and Policy Making. Paper presented to the Norman Thomas Symposium, Vanderbilt University, Sept. 30–Oct. 3.

Sniderman, Paul M., Richard A. Brody, and Philip E. Tetlock. 1991. *Reasoning and Choice: Explorations in Political Psychology.* New York: Cambridge University Press.

Soley, Lawrence. 1992. *The News Shapers: The Sources Who Explain the News.* New York: Praeger.

Steel, Ronald. 1980. *Walter Lippmann and the American Century.* Boston: Little, Brown.

Talese, Gay. 1970. *The Kingdom and the Power.* New York: Bantam.

Times Mirror Center for the People and the Press. 1993. The Vocal Minority in American Politics. Press release, July 16.

Tuchman, Gaye. 1978. *Making News: A Study in the Construction of Reality.* New York: Free Press.

Turow, Joseph. 1974. Talk Show Radio as Interpersonal Communication. *Journal of Broadcasting* 18(2): 171–79.

Vanderbilt Television News Archive. 1993. *Television News Index and Abstracts.* January.

Viles, Peter. 1992. Talkers Let Fly on Check-Bouncing Scandal. *Broadcasting*, March 23, 76.

Winters, Jeffrey. 1995. *Power in Motion.* Ithaca, N.Y.: Cornell University Press.

Woodward, Bob. 1994. *The Agenda: Inside the Clinton White House.* New York: Simon and Schuster.

Zaller, John R. 1992. *The Nature and Origins of Mass Opinion.* New York: Cambridge University Press.

Zane, Peder. 1995. Now, the Magazines of "Me." *New York Times,* May 14, sec. 4, 4.